7

JAZZ IN BRITAIN

JAZZ

IN

B

BY

DAVID BOULTON

Foreword by CHRIS BARBER

RITAIN

W. H. ALLEN LONDON 1958

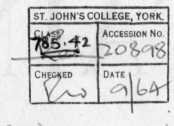
Printed in Great Britain by
T. & A. Constable Ltd., Hopetoun Street, Edinburgh
for the publishers, W. H. Allen & Co. Ltd., Essex Street, London, WC2

For M *and* D
and ml

ACKNOWLEDGEMENTS

ACKNOWLEDGEMENTS are due to Sylvia Paddock and Lily Boulton for secretarial assistance; Brian Nicholls for supplying much factual information on present-day British bands; E.M.I. Ltd. for permission to use their photograph of the O.D.J.B.; the *Dancing Times* for permission to use the photographs of the Original Lyrical Five and the Hammersmith Palais de Danse; and the *Melody Maker* for generously opening its files for inspection and free use.

AUTHOR'S NOTE

No historian, set the task of writing a complete history of England, would start his saga at the reign of James II. If he tried, his story would be obviously unbalanced; it would give all sorts of wrong impressions, and the author would constantly find that in order to give the full meaning to certain events it was necessary to refer back, in explanation, to others that occurred long before his self-imposed starting-line. In short, the only sensible place to begin a thing is at the beginning.

But jazz critics writing of British jazz have often disputed this, in deed if not in word. They have started the story of British jazz with George Webb's Dixielanders, the band which sparked off the New Orleans revival in this country during the last war. Now the Dixielanders *did* make a second start; but the accent is on the second.

Of course, there was very little in the way of British jazz, as the purist understands the term, before 1943. But it is indefensible, sticking even to the narrowest terms of reference, to claim that there was none at all. And there was certainly a great deal of music labelled "jazz", some of it very much more worth while, and very much nearer the genuine spirit of jazz as we now understand it, than a number of critics would have us believe.

I have written of jazz in Britain. There is a lot of difference between that and British jazz. There was, before the '40s, nothing in the jazz line that was distinctively British. (It is arguable, of course, whether there has been any since.) My story, then, is one of a whole succession of American invasions, punctuating the British field of popular music; of misunderstanding, of alternating revival and decline.

It is intended for the general reader who feels attracted to a story of change and decay; for the jazz enthusiast who knows his Ramsay, Jnr. and his Harris; and for those who want a record of jazz in Britain, past and present.

CONTENTS

ILLUSTRATIONS

FOREWORD

JAZZ has been in existence now for some sixty years in forms recognisably similar to those which can be heard at the present time.

It first came to light in and around New Orleans, Louisiana, near the end of the last century, and it took nearly twenty years for a fully fledged jazz band to reach these shores. It has taken some forty years more for jazz in Britain to reach a level of popularity and artistic worth which could lead to the writing and publication of this book.

"Jazz" is probably the most misused word in the dictionary—perhaps because, like most creative art-forms, it is very hard to define and harder still to justify in the face of those people who simply see no point in it!

No doubt to some of you it will conjure up a mental picture of a Charleston band bashing at a "jazz kit"; to others, Louis Armstrong playing at the Palladium in 1932; and, finally, no doubt there are some who will see visions of dark and dirty cellars complete with drunken orgies and perhaps even "dope".

I picked up this book with the intention merely of taking a preliminary glance at it at 4 a.m. one morning, on arrival home from an engagement outside London. At 7 a.m. I finally put it down, having read it from cover to cover.

In the course of some fifteen years as a jazz enthusiast and musician I have amassed quite a considerable knowledge of the story of British jazz, but I grew up in the post-war era when there was at no time an American jazz band to hear and learn from. My contemporaries and I have had to pick up what we could from old recordings rather than being influenced by recent trends in jazz in its birthplace.

This book not only set out for me the events which I already know of, but also gave me for the first time a great deal of information about the earlier attempts to play jazz here and the American influences behind them. The author shows how, without any such intention, my contemporaries and I seem to have established an English style of jazz. I must admit to being somewhat surprised and flattered by his description of myself as "historically the Bix Beiderbecke of English jazz", but I must also admit that his reasoning is persuasive.

I am glad to see also that David Boulton does not (as do a number of other experts) condemn skiffle as something either worthless or horrible.

I personally must confess to having had a considerable hand in the establishing of skiffle on the English popular scene and I do not regret it. I cannot see the appearance of such wonderful material as "Bring a little water, Sylvie", "John Henry" and "Lost John" on the Hit Parade as anything short of a miracle—and a very pleasant one at that!

It seems to me that jazz, having spread so widely across this country (and, indeed, the rest of the world), can never really vanish again. It is a style of music capable of so many shades of feeling and mood that whatever the general mood of the populace it must be possible to entertain them with a varied performance in the jazz idiom. I would like to take this opportunity of wishing it a long and happy future and of thanking David Boulton for uncovering so much of the background which led to its present popularity and also for his penetrating analysis of the present-day situation.

CHRIS BARBER

LONDON, *January* 1958

I

FOUR DECADES OF JAZZ IN BRITAIN

Chapter 1

THE BACKGROUND

The music now known universally as jazz developed when the folk-music of the American Negro came into contact with, and began to assimilate, the "European" music of white American society. New Orleans was the home of most of the musicians who had any part in creating "classic" jazz, but, for economic reasons, most of these musicians were dispersed immediately before and during World War I. In 1915, Tom Brown's Band from Dixieland, playing in Chicago, first attracted the use of the slang term "jazz" to describe its music.

IN the year 1441 Antão Goncalves, a prosperous Portuguese merchant, making a bold attempt to keep up with the fifteenth-century Joneses in both prestige and prosperity, shipped to his homeland a cargo of Negro slaves.

The seed that was to flower as jazz was sown.

By the advent of the sixteenth century many thousands of Africans were being dragged from their Dark Continent into the slavery of more enlightened lands. The Portuguese pioneers were followed by the Dutch and the British, and soon by almost the whole of Europe, the trade being stimulated by the opening up of new markets in Brazil. Treated on the crossing like animals, many died like animals long before the New World was sighted. Those who survived may well have envied their less hardy brethren.

Early in the seventeenth century the first batch of slaves was introduced into the Southern States of the English-American colonies. Rapid development of the area accelerated the traffic, and between 1680 and 1780 over two million Negroes were imported specifically for slave labour. A tremendous boost was given to the trade by the invention of the "cotton-gin" in 1793, which led to more rapid production, consequent expansion of area planted and a greater demand for cheap labour. The slave population was to rise, eventually, beyond the three and a half million mark.

Slaves never had more than the most drastically limited personal rights; in some cases they had none at all. If Mrs. Stowe can be written off as a sentimentalist, it is none the less true that husbands WERE separated from wives, and mothers from children, on such occasions as the white master found the separation financially attractive. Some were made to live like cattle and were worked equally hard, and although theoretically it was possible to obtain freedom after certain conditions of service had been fulfilled, in practice individual emancipation was rarely granted or expected.

In spite of their condition, living in an alien land where contempt and hatred, broken hearts and broken backs were integral parts of the system, the Negroes managed to retain their finest characteristics. In spite of that great curtain of melancholy which later permeated the music that they made, they never lost their infinite capacity for joy and the exuberant lust for life that has dominated their history.

Towards the end of the eighteenth century the British conscience, quickened by the indignant preaching of the Evangelicals, revolted against the whole slavery set-up and demanded changes which led eventually to the reforms introduced by Wilberforce. The British attitude was soon reflected in the consciences of the settlers in the Northern States, and this, coupled with a less praiseworthy insistence on seeing one great undivided American nation centrally governed in the North, led eventually to civil war. In 1863 Abraham Lincoln, victorious leader of the North, issued a proclamation which freed well over two million slaves, and two years later, when the 13th Amendment to the Constitution was finally adopted, all Negro peoples became as free—in the eyes of the law—as their erstwhile owners.

In the eyes of the law. But the law is no more than an abstraction, and victory won by the spilling of blood is no victory. Freed from the plantations and finding little restriction on travelling, the Negro attempted to improve his lot in the cities of the North and West or the Mississippi townships. Here he found only the lowest grades of manual labour available to him; he was the first to be unemployed. Before long the short-lived franchisement that he had enjoyed was retracted; segregation laws came into force; legal representation was denied him and lynchings became regular occurrences. Rent rose to double that charged to whites, resulting in the appropriation of Negro slum sites and the rise of a community within a community where social life tended to divorce itself from outside influences and to develop along its own lines according to its own inner logic.

In the Place de Nègres, New Orleans, traditional Negro dances continued to be performed, and the Place was nicknamed "Congo Square". These dances were no longer the barbaric and sensual affairs that they had once been, but they were nevertheless sufficiently different from anything of their kind and sufficiently bizarre and colourful to have a considerable influence on the social music which was developing in the Negro quarters of the city, and particularly in that area in the centre of the city known as "*Story*ville", after a City Councillor of that name who had persuaded his colleagues that, since vice and prostitution could never be eliminated in so large a community, it would be best controlled if restricted to a proscribed area. Other influences were also brought to bear upon this music. A form of syncopated quadrille developed by Negro pianists further along the Mississippi which had achieved sudden spectacular fame at the Chicago World's Fair of 1898, where it was called "ragtime", had within a few years swept America, leaving an indelible imprint on the sweet and jaded dance music which had until then characterised the more sophisticated ball-rooms, and the new style was taken over, lock, stock and barrel, by the New Orleans Negro quarter. Again, the Crescent City (so-called after the Mississippi curve in which the city sits) was as cosmopolitan as any place in the world, and Spanish, French, English and Celtic characteristics became woven into the general fabric of the now distinctive New Orleans music.

Other roots stretched further back into the Negro's own past. Few races have developed so rich a body of folk-song as they; plantation work-songs, community chants and ballad-narratives of incredible variety have been an inexhaustible source of the various schools of music that were to follow. When, after the Civil War, the Baptist and Methodist Churches had sponsored Evangelistic Campaigns and Revival Meetings for Negro congregations, introducing to them the simple Moody-Sankey-type hymns, the congregations had quickly picked them up and transformed them according to their own musical traditions, producing the spiritual. As economic conditions began to change, a class of professional minstrels, calling themselves "music physicianers", came into being and earned their living, as had their medieval counterparts in Europe, by travelling from settlement to settlement, singing to their own banjo or guitar accompaniment. Gradually consolidating the diffuse tradition upon which they drew, they produced what may well prove to have been the most powerful and compelling form to have developed within the confines of folk-music: the blues. Difficult to define accurately, the blues may be described as a ballad or secular spiritual, the music of which is set in a unique tension between the European equal-temperament scales and the ancient pentatonic, or five-note, scale common to much of the world's folk-music. Utterly disregarding the European virtues of tonal purity and sweet harmony, the aim of the blues singer is to communicate emotion rather than any preconceived notion of beauty. The controlled voice-distortions, the micro-tonal flattening and "dirty-toned" glissandi would hardly find favour at Glyndebourne,

22

but they contributed a great deal towards making the social music of New Orleans a unique organisation of sounds.

Perhaps no city in the world was more "organisation-minded" than the musical mecca of the South. Practically everyone seems to have belonged to several clubs, brotherhoods, secret orders and societies, many of which had no function to perform other than that of arranging the occasional "get-together" calling for musical celebration. Brass bands were formed for street parades, and by the turn of the century these were very much under the influence of the blues and ragtime, producing a "Hot Style" of marching music in which improvisation played an important part. Possibly the first and certainly the most famous of these was the band led by "King" Buddy Bolden, a Negro barber. With fellow cornet man Willie "Bunk" Johnson, trombonists Willie Cornish and Frankie Dusen and clarinettist Frank Lewis, Bolden created a reputation that was second to none, whether playing for the public dances organised in the Tin Type Mortuary or parading in Lincoln Park. It has been variously asserted that his cornet could be heard two, eight and even ten miles away: Morton insists that it was fourteen!

In 1904 he entered a lunatic asylum, which he never left during his remaining thirty years. He blew his brains right through that horn, they said.

Although the new music originated and matured in the Negro sector, it attracted no little attention from the local whites. Well before Bolden lost his reason and handed over control of his band to Dusen, drummer Jack Laine was organising a similar group and playing similar music. With Lawrence Vegas (cornet), Achille Baquet (clarinet), Dave Perkins (trombone), Willie Guitar (string bass) and Morton Abraham (guitar), Laine became the king of white New Orleans—the white man's Bolden. In 1908 Tom "Red" Brown formed Brown's Ragtime Band, a combination which was to earn the distinction of being the first native New Orleans group to introduce their "Dixieland" music to Chicago. Also in 1908, white cornetist Nick La Rocca formed his first group, La Rocca's Ragtime Band, at a time when such names as Keppard, Oliver, Morton, Marable, Bechet and "Big Eye" Nelson were beginning to mean something in local musical circles.

In and around the city the new ragtime-and-blues style continued to develop, with Storyville as unofficial research centre, since, where the best money was to be found, there the best musicians claimed it. As war was breaking out in Europe, New Orleans music was beginning to crystallise into a definite style. The basis was collective improvisation on a theme; solos were few and far between, and the accent was on volume rather than dynamic subtlety. The form of any particular piece was rarely more complicated than a statement/improvisation/concerted-statement sequence, sometimes furnished with an introduction after the manner of the quadrille, and a coda. And the music was still quite unnoticed by the vast majority of straight musicians and indeed any self-respecting portion of the public. When at last people did begin to sit up and take notice it was a white group that attracted attention; and its audience was a long, long way from New Orleans.

As we have seen, it was trombonist Tom Brown who first transplanted the music of the Crescent City northwards to the Windy City. Arriving early in 1915 with colleagues Ray Lopez on cornet, Gus Mueller on clarinet, William Lambert on drums and Arnold Loyocano hovering between string bass and piano, Brown received an immediate invitation to play at Lamb's Café, where he opened in June, being billed as Tom Brown's Band from Dixieland. His stay there made history; an official of the local musicians' union, anxious that the visitors would not outshine home-grown talent (evidently an occupational disease of musicians' unions), smeared the new group by denouncing them as a "real jass band". The word "jass" was a Chicago epithet with obscene associations, and the people flocked in their hundreds to find out for themselves just what obscene music sounded like. Business boomed at Lamb's and the management delightedly billed its musicians as Brown's Dixieland Jass Band, and before long "jass" bands were sprouting up all over the city.

In 1916 La Rocca arrived in Chicago with his new Dixie Land Jass Band, consisting of Alcide "Yellow" Nunez on clarinet, Eddie Edwards on trombone, Henry Ragas on piano, Tony Sbarbaro on drums, and La Rocca himself playing cornet lead. Their engagement was at Schiller's Café, where they soon became the biggest rivals of Tom Brown's band, and after trading Nunez for Brown's new clarinettist Larry Shields, who had a few months earlier replaced Gus Mueller, La Rocca's men forced the rival Dixieland Jass firm to leave Lamb's and reorganise as the Tom Brown Band, later to make a come-back as the Louisiana Five. Within a few months the Dixie Land Jass Band itself deserted Chicago and set out for the as yet unconquered fields of New York, and it was here, operating from Reisenweber's Café in Columbus Circle, that they became the first New Orleans band to obtain a national reputation. When, in 1917, cornetist Freddie Keppard refused to allow his Original Creole Orchestra to cut records for Victor, in the belief that playing the discs would deprive him of work and make it all too easy for rivals to copy his style, the company approached the Dixie Land Band, who made "Dixie Jass Band One-Step", "Livery Stable Blues", "Tiger Rag" and a stream of others, again revising their title and calling themselves the Original Dixieland Jass Band and finally the Original Dixieland Jazz Band.

Back in New Orleans the jazz scene—as we may now call it—was in a ferment. Ever since Tom Brown had struck out for Chicago, a growing trickle of musicians had been uprooting themselves and seeking fame and fortune in the same direction. The trickle was augmented by a number who were finding Storyville a less and less pleasant place to work, as violent crime rocketed sky-high, reflecting the new war-time uncertainty. Out in the country the cotton-boll weevil was ravaging large areas of Louisiana, Mississippi, Alabama, Georgia and Florida, and unusually high flooding by the Mississippi River and its tributaries had helped swell the stream of labourers moving into the towns. In Storyville, tempers rose in proportion to population. "There were an awful lot of killings going on," Louis Armstrong tells us, "—mysterious ones too. . . . Several sailors were all messed up—robbed and killed. . . . Those prostitutes commenced to having their pimps hide somewheres around and either rob—or bash their brains in—anything to get that money."[1] The Navy Department of the Federal Government decided that the area was causing more trouble than it had been designed to prevent, and they eventually decided, in spite of the indignant protests of the city government, that the vice-spots would have to be cleaned up, the area reverting to the same legal status as the rest of the city. In went the navy—and out came the good-time girls to the strains of massed bands playing "Nearer, my God, to Thee". Musicians were faced with the choice of either returning to the trades they had long since deserted for the easy money of Storyville, or moving North. The best of them took the latter course.

"So we turned out nice and reformed," adds Armstrong.

Attempts have been made to glorify Storyville as a lusty, lazy, Rabelaisian, romantic sort of place. The plain truth is that it was sordid, brutal and vicious; human life was of little account and ethical standards were as low as the thickest string of a string bass. That jazz matured and flourished in this place, that good came out of evil, we cannot doubt; but those who insist that sex and sin were necessary catalysts underestimate the irrepressible potency of a force which,

---

[1] Quoted from *Hear Me Talkin' To Ya*, edited by Nat Shapiro and Nat Hentoff.

although it was shaped by them, was not by any means wholly dependent upon outside factors.

The primary colours of our background have now been painted in. With the closing of Storyville, New Orleans folk-music, as such, began to decline; the conditions that had brought it into being no longer obtained and the best of the city's musicians had moved out. But jazz was too young to die; its unexplored backwaters continued to flourish, one in Negro churches throughout the South and another in the local village brass bands. And more important—for our purpose —than either of these, commencing with the New York success of the Original Dixieland Jazz Band and the coronation of Joe Oliver as "King" of jazz in Chicago, the music entered into its universal phase as the unique stuff that fits no pigeon-hole. Less inhibited and more direct than art music, less anonymous and more self-conscious than folk-music, jazz was now that rarity of rarities, something new under the sun.

Chapter 2

JAZZ IN CARICATURE

The caricaturing of the American Negro was a popular Victorian pastime, both here and across the Atlantic. The "Nigger Minstrel" shows thus helped to create a spurious "comic-hat" attitude toward all entertainment from that quarter. Negro spirituals also achieved remarkable popularity in sentimental white-washed versions. In 1912 syncopated dance music arrived in Britain via America, under the "ragtime" label. It swept the country for the next five years, giving rise to novelty bands and a renewal of the "comic-hat" tradition. By 1917 the name jazz began to succeed ragtime.

THE serious study of folk-music has been a twentieth-century pastime. Certainly, in Victorian times, the unhealthy veneration of music and art had the effect of damning the less-pretentious stuff as primitive and insignificant, and in England, as on the Continent, industrialisation was killing the traditional muse of men of the soil. It was not until Holst and Vaughan Williams rediscovered in English folk-song and folk-dance qualities which enabled them to break free from the Parry/Stanford/Elgar cul-de-sac that the music, of its own right, began to attract attention to itself; and it was left to an Englishman, Frederick Delius, and a Bohemian, Antonin Dvořák, to show the Americans that there was, on their own doorstep, an inexhaustible spring waiting to be tapped. Folk-music in Europe was dying; traditional musical phrases falling from human lips were replaced by factory smoke belching from brick chimneys. But in the New World the tradition was very much alive; and it was going unnoticed.

Unnoticed, at any rate, in the academic conservatoires. But even before the Civil War the Negro plantation music was providing a source of material for the entertainment world, and during the 1840s much of it was presented, in a caricatured form, by groups of white "minstrels" who blackened their faces, imitated (or attempted to imitate) Negro peculiarities of speech and generally amused their audiences by "nigger-baiting". In 1848 one of the pioneering groups calling themselves Major Dumbledon's Ethiopian Serenaders visited London, bringing with them a repertoire of "most bewitching melodies of Ethiopian and African origin", and the impact that they made influenced the British attitude towards American Negro music for the next seventy years. They were soon followed by the New Orleans Serenaders, who maintained the Dumbledon tradition, and finally, just as Lincoln's forces were proving themselves the stronger, Stephen Collins Foster brought over his famous Christy Minstrels.

Although born in Pittsburgh, Foster had spent most of his life in the slave States. He was an accomplished song-writer, attracted by the vein of melancholy in Negro music rather than the "funny stuff", and most of his songs played on the nostalgic yearnings of his audiences rather than on any sense of humour. London welcomed him with open arms; his sentimentality was admirably suited to Victorian tastes, and within a month of his arrival the whole country was singing his "Swannee River":

> All up and down de whole creation
>   Sadly I roam,
> Still longing for de old plantation
>   And for de old folks at home. . . .
>
> One little hut among de bushes—
>   One dat I love—
> Still sadly to my mem'ry rushes,
>   No matter where I rove.

When will I see de bees a-humming
All round de comb?
When will I hear de banjo tumming
Down in de good old home?

All de world am sad and dreary . . .

The Christy Minstrels developed their entertainment to a fine art. Their performances were divided into three "acts"; the First Part, the Ohio and the Afterpiece. The First Part usually opened with a concerted musical number, the members of the troupe being seated in an open semicircle facing the audience, and the interlocutor or master of ceremonies standing in the centre. Individual members were then called upon to sing or dance, the two end-men, "Bones" and "Tambo", providing a continuous nonsensical patter. The Ohio was a little more elaborate, often an inconsequential grouping together of singing, dancing and novelty acts with nonsense "stump speeches". The Afterpiece was dramatic farce of little musical interest. This pattern was also adopted by other visiting troupes such as Buckley's Serenaders, the Old Folks and the Colored Opera Troupe, and was taken over by the amateur "Nigger Minstrels" that began to spring up all over the country. So numerous were these latter that a collection of Minstrel Songs was published in 1861. "Negro Minstrelsy," we read in the Preface, "instead of relaxing its hold on the interest and sympathy of the British public, has yearly increased in popularity until at length it may be truly said to have become permanently established in the favour of all classes of society."

Thomas Rice, another native of Pittsburgh, also contributed a great deal to the British conception of the Negro. As early as the 1820s Rice became famous after witnessing, from a window at the back of a Pittsburgh theatre, the strange behaviour of an old Negro cripple who was performing a grotesque dance in which the bodily contortions were punctuated with snatches of song:

Wheel about, turn about,
Jump jes' so;
And every time I turn about
I call "Jim Crow".

Rice imitated the "dance", added verses to the "song" and hit the headlines with his new act. "Jim Crow" novelties flooded the shops as Mickey Mouse and Dan Dare novelties were to do a century later, and the song and dance are still to be found as part of a children's game. When the segregation laws came into force the bus services, park benches and churches set apart for the Negro became known as "Jim Crow", and the term is as topical today as ever it was. But the point is that an Englishman's idea of the American Negro's music was entirely dependent upon the impression given by the white minstrels and the comic "Jim Crow" dance.

This state of affairs lasted until 1873, when the first all-Negro band arrived in London in the shape of eight singers, all members of the Fisk University, Nashville, Tennessee, which had the distinction of being the first Negro school to be opened after Emancipation. In order to raise the funds that were necessary to keep the school functioning, the octet, calling themselves the "Jubilee Singers", had toured churches and concert-halls in America, singing the spirituals and religious songs of slavery days. Now they were in England, and England was enchanted. Queen Victoria, Gladstone and the Earl of Shaftesbury all heard and praised them. "Steal Away Home" and "Swing Low" joined "Swannee River" and "Down in de Canebreak" as popular classics, and such was the general furore that even the musical fraternity were forced to sit up and take notice. The "complicated and sometimes strikingly original" rhythms were noted and the "entire absence of triple time or three-part measure" commented upon. One celebrated critic gave it as his opinion that the spirituals were "never composed after the manner of ordinary music", suggesting that they "sprang into life, ready made, from the white heat of religious fervour during some protracted meeting in church or camp", and that "they come from no musical cultivation whatever but are the simple, ecstatic utterances of wholly untutored minds. From so unpromising a source we could reasonably expect only such a mass of crudities as would be unendurable to the cultivated ear. On the contrary, however, the cultivated listener confesses to a new charm, and to a power never before felt, at least in kind."

This was a sweeping change of attitude, and for the next quarter of a century Negro music was understood as a combination of cheap comedy and religious sentiment. Music publishers seized on the spirituals, printed them in the now familiar "nice and glossy" versions and churned them out with the drawing-room ballads. Everyone simply *adored* them.

Quite suddenly, in 1912, the centre of imported American music switched dramatically from the drawing-room to the ball-room. On September 23rd the Original American Ragtime Octette created a sensation at the London Hippodrome and sparked off the revolution which slowly swept away the "sweet" dance orchestras and replaced them with the small, compact syncopated bands. The songs they introduced—"Ragtime Cowboy Joe", "Mysterious Rag", and the most successful of all, "Alexander's Ragtime Band"— swept away the old "coon" songs and established "ragtime" as a household word. An initial engagement of six weeks was extended "by popular request"; the Octette made tour after tour of the provinces; and not until 1917 did they return to America. The hotels, restaurants and clubs of the West End were forced to take no scant notice of the new trends, and as early as 1912 Ciro's Club was featuring a coloured combination, and Murray's engaged the coloured Versatile Three, featuring a comic-hat ragtime style.

The First World War came; syncopation remained. "The officers and men of the British Army when home on leave from the front often obtained relaxation from the horrors and hardships of the

The Original Dixieland Jazz Band as they appeared in Britain in 1919.

Left to right: Billy Jones (p), Larry Shields (cl), Nick La Rocca (co), Emil Christian (tb), Tony Sbarbaro (ds).

The Hammersmith Palais de Danse as it appeared when opened by the Original Dixieland Jazz Band in 1919.

The "Original Lyrical Five" re-created the music of the Original Dixieland Jazz Band for a few weeks at the Palais de Danse in 1923.

trenches by the help of this musical alcohol. They needed a powerful stimulant, and the strong rhythms and the bright colours of the syncopated dance orchestra gave it to them. . . . It may have been a superficial excitement, but it was real nevertheless, and it did much to ease the tension."[1]

Before the war was over, and within a year of its being applied to Brown's Dixieland Band in Chicago, the word "jazz" began to supersede "ragtime" and "syncopation" in British dance-music terminology. The music to which it was applied would not be given the name today, but it was, nevertheless, a few steps nearer the music of New Orleans. "Five instruments form the foundation of a true 'Jazz Band', namely the clarinet (playing violin parts), the cornet, the trombone, a 'snappy' drummer, and a ragtime piano-player. To these are often added banjos, banjorines and a stringed bass." So advised the *Dancing Times*, then in the forefront of musical journalism, and it was not far wrong. The word "jazz" itself created a great deal of interest, and various theories were tentatively advanced regarding its origin. It was suggested that it was first used in American mining camps in the Wild West and taken over by "niggers on the move", and again that the term had been borrowed from a Chinese Joss Orchestra in San Francisco.[2]

The new music had a mixed reception. "Jazz music is the latest terror from the States," complained one jaded critic. "It has been described as the delirium tremens of syncopation. It is strict rhythm without melody. . . . There are many half-notes or less and many long-drawn wavering notes. It is an attempt to reproduce the marvellous syncopation of the African jungle." The musical director at the Coliseum defined it as "a piece of music entirely surrounded by noise", and another critic found it unnecessary to attempt any definition since "most people know what jazz is; it is almost impossible to

[1] R. W. S. Mendl's *The Appeal of Jazz*, 1925.
[2] See Appendix I.

describe its motions in print, for obvious reasons". On the other hand, the voice of reason was occasionally heard: "We are authoritatively assured that 'Jazz' is not music, but merely noise. However, as exactly the same thing was said of Wagner's music when it came to birth, it is possible that the process of time may change the critical pronouncement as to 'Jazz'. If it finds a definite place among our musical literature despite the cavilling of the ultra-analytic, it shall be counted to its creators as music."

But this modicum of understanding did not last long. In March 1918, dancing mistress Egerton Welch announced that she was exhibiting and teaching three of New York's latest crazes—the "Ramble", the "Three-Step" and (printed most prominently in the advertisements) the "Jazz". Within weeks her colleagues were doing much the same thing and the public began to look upon jazz as nothing more than the last in a long line of short-lived novelty dance-steps, accompanied by crazy music. New Dancing Schools were opened for the specific purpose of teaching the "Jazz", the "Jazz-Roll", the "Jazz-Step" and the "Shimmy-Jazz", and the Herman Darewski Music Publishing Company published an instructional "Jazz Chart". This misconception, backed as it was by "big business", flourished for nearly three years; nor did it diminish when Mrs. Vernon Castle, acknowledged as "perhaps the most celebrated of all ball-room dancers", roundly asserted that "on one point I am definite; there is no such dance as the 'Jazz', and anyone who tells you there is is wrong. . . . The nigger bands at home 'Jazz' a tune: that is to say, they slur the notes, they syncopate, and each instrument puts in a lot of little fancy bits of its own. . . . I have not come across a 'Jazz' Band in England, and I doubt if there is one."[1]

There may have been no genuine jazz band in the country, but there were nevertheless a hundred and one groups claiming to be such. The first was the Murray Club Jazz Band formed towards the

[1] *Dancing Times*, November 1918.

end of 1917, and it was followed by Alfred Delmonte's Jazz Band, the Boston Jazz Band, Billy Tell's Jazz Band and the Indianola Jazz Band. These groups featured a "syncopation-gone-mad" mode of music, striving to outdo each other in the noisiness of their noise and the novelty of the effects they employed. There was about as much Negro colouring in their music as there is Turkish colouring in Mozart's "Seraglio" choruses, and as much blues feeling as in Walton's setting of the Sitwell "Trio for two Cats and a Trombone".

And the consequence was that when the real thing arrived it was written off as "just another jazz band".

Chapter 3

CURTAIN UP

On top of the ragtime craze the Original Dixieland Jazz Band introduced genuine jazz to Britain at the newly opened Hammersmith Palais. Before long they were falling into line with the current British demand for novelty music presented in comedy manner. A number of native musicians imitated the new "Dixieland" style, other American bands arrived in London, and the new style of jazz spread throughout the country. It was soon condemned as "a menace to morals".

IN 1919 the Original Dixieland Jazz Band arrived in London. Having conquered America by means of their recordings and their sensational success at Reisenweber's in New York, they were hungry for new fields of conquest. Britain supplied them, and to Britain they came, bringing with them a music richly steeped in the New Orleans tradition and reflecting many of the characteristics of Oliver, Dodds and Ory, whom they had heard before leaving Chicago. Pianist Henry Ragas had died only a month before their departure and had been replaced by New York ragtime man J. Russell Robinson. Trombonist Eddie Edwards, being unable or unwilling to make the journey to Europe, was succeeded by Emil Christian. La Rocca remained on cornet, Larry Shields on clarinet and Tony Sbarbaro on drums.

Their first engagement was at the London Hippodrome, where they were given a fifteen-minute spot in de Courville's revue "Joy Bells". They could hardly have chosen a more inopportune time to introduce their wares to the British public. Reaction against what was thought to be jazz was then at its highest, and George Robey had little difficulty in persuading the "Joy Bells" producers to scrap the offending item. The O.D.J.B. lasted one night only, and for a while its activities were restricted to late-night work at Marten's Club. It was only when they moved to Rector's that the general public began to notice that here was something very different from the bang-crash stuff to be heard at Murray's and elsewhere in the West End.

When, in the autumn of 1919, the magnificent Palais de Danse was opened at Hammersmith, it was the Original Dixielanders who were engaged as resident band, along with a New York bang-crash group, Billy Arnold's American Novelty Jazz Band, who subsequently faded into the background, embarked on a tour of France and then apparently disappeared without trace. The Dixielanders threw over their New York label—"Untuneful Harmonists playing Peppery Melodies"—and billed themselves, with no more truth but a little more dignity, "The Creators of Jazz". Their success has been described as "unprecedented" and "sensational", but how much of it was due to the music they played and how much to the attraction of a brand-new luxury ball-room it is hard to tell. Neither the La Rocca nor the Arnold group seem to have been considered particularly news-worthy by the press, which paid a great deal of attention to the layout, general architecture, staffing and policy of the Palais. Even the *Dancing Times*, the earliest forum for jazz controversy, never found the Dixielanders worth the barest mention, and the Palais management, embarking on what was then an ambitious advertising scheme, did little more than mention that they were employing "two celebrated Jazz Bands playing pleasing Dance Music—

> " ' When Henry the Eighth was on the throne
> And lodged his wives at Hampton Court,
> A Morris Dance to the fiddler's drone
> No doubt he would consider was ripping sport.

But if today he did return,
A mortal of these lands,
At the Palais de Danse he soon would learn
To dance to the two Jazz Bands.'"

It has very often been implied, in articles and books on jazz, that the Original Dixieland Jazz Band burst upon London and swept it off its feet with the sheer vitality and originality of jazz music. I have been at pains to show that the very reverse was the case: that the band arrived in a London bowed down with various prejudices for and against what it believed to be jazz, and that the real sensation of its impact was felt only some years later when it had achieved the status of an historical monument and its influences were beginning to be appreciated. Another misconception of more recent origin which has found its way even into so reliable a book as Rex Harris's Penguin *Jazz*, has been the idea that it was the comedy-presentation of the band which was responsible for the delay of over two decades before anything more than a tiny minority of the public began to consider the music seriously. Thus, "What musical purity the O.D.J.B. possessed was lost in a wild helter-skelter of trombones played with the feet, fancy hats, and saucepan-lid drum kits. . . . The sad part of this turn of events is that the travesty of the truth prevails today and the blind prejudice felt by many towards *what they think* is jazz can be traced straight back to the Original Dixieland Jazz Band's comic hats." But we must not stop there. The Original Dixielanders borrowed their novelty antics from the British jazz bands preceding them. They fell into line with current public taste, but they did not, in the first place, create it.

It has been suggested that the band had no influence on British musicians until, in the late '20s and '30s, its records became collectors' items. But more than one player of fame or fortune in subsequent years has claimed that initially his imagination was fired by hearing them in the flesh, and Lew Davis, who became particularly prominent as first trombone in Lew Stone's Orchestra during the middle '30s, has left it on record that his very first experience of jazz was the "Joy Bells" debut. "They started playing when the curtain was still down," he tells us, "and from the first note I felt strangely stirred and exhilarated."[1] So much so, that the following day he purchased a decaying trombone from a second-hand store and commenced to teach himself the tailgate style of Emil Christian. He was to do much to keep the Dixieland style alive during the subsequent jazz depression, and at one time attempted to form a native band directly modelled on the O.D.J.B. consisting of himself on trombone, Syd Roy on piano and Harry Roy on clarinet and soprano, backed by two banjorines and drums. But the Lyricals was a short-lived group; the public were not ready for it, and true jazz remained the prerogative of a handful of enthusiastic amateurs.

After a few months Russell Robinson left La Rocca and returned to the States, and after playing for a few nights as a quartet, British ragtime pianist Billy Jones was added. He remained with them until the end of their tour, after which he seems to have taken a back seat as far as the musical scene at home is concerned, reappearing in 1935 (as, by coincidence, did his colleagues back in America) to make some records with his own Dixieland Band. Until recently he owned a public-house in Chelsea, but his piano was by no means forsaken, or used only for accumulating beer-mugs.

The O.D.J.B. was followed by other American bands with various shades of jazz interest. Art Hickman's New York-London Five opened at the Criterion Roof and were followed by the Louisiana Jazz Band, the Paramount Six, the Manhattan Five (reputedly the first jazz band to be heard on the "wireless"), Billy Madden's Crescent City Orchestra and the Jazz Kings—the latter being the first all-coloured combination since the pre-jazz ragtime days. None of these was in the top class,

[1] *Melody Maker*, July 2nd, 1934.

but they did keep before the public some basic ideas regarding what jazz was and what it was not.

Anything new thrives on controversy. The early arguments as to whether jazz was a dance-step, a method of playing or a Doctor-Crock-and-his-Crackpots music resolved themselves into a relatively simple but nevertheless bitter struggle of Anti and Pro camps. With the former were ranged the vested interests of "sweet" music and the whole army of more serious concert music—this at a time when Stanford was still venerated and Schoenberg was generally written off as an irresponsible eccentric—large sections of the Church, and the older generation almost *en masse*. Of the two camps, the Anti-faction was by far the most vociferous, consequently gaining more publicity in the daily press, where it was announced as "degrading to encourage the dance of low niggers in America", or, as another theory of origins had it, the "grotesque and indecent movements invented by drunken cowboys in the Argentine". Jazz music was considered a menace to morals, and wise parents were advised to keep their daughters well away from it, in much the same manner as they themselves had been protected from the now innocuous waltz.[1]

On the strictly musical side, jazz was sneered at for its "appalling crudity". Members of the legitimate music profession could never forget that not one of the Original Dixielanders was able to read music. La Rocca's habit of turning to the band, rattling off the first few notes of the tune he wanted them to play and giving a "one-two-away" signal with his foot, was not one to appeal to the sophisticated. "Collective improvisation" was a term virtually unknown in the academies, and improvisation of any sort was of interest only as a moribund relic of Handelian opera, concerto cadenzas and harpsichord obbligati. That jazz, as introduced by the O.D.J.B., possessed few of the attributes considered by convention to be essential to good

[1] See Appendix I.

music was all too obvious. That it must needs be judged on its own merits and evaluated on an entirely new basis peculiar to itself was not.

So the curtain arose on jazz in Britain; seeds were sown; the ball was set rolling.

Chapter 4

DECLINE AND REVIVAL

"Dixieland" jazz appeared to be on the decline by 1921. Paul Whiteman, by his recordings and by a visit in 1923, spread the gospel of symphonic syncopation. Jazz began to be recognised as a progressive music. In 1927 the first British book on jazz was published. Records made by New York groups heralded the revival of a neo-Dixieland or "hot" jazz. Fred Elizalde led a live "hot" group at Cambridge, and later at London's Savoy Hotel, becoming the accepted leader of the jazz avant-garde *of the 'twenties. By articles in the* Melody Maker *he introduced a number of American stars to the British public.*

THE full story of the meanderings of jazz in Britain during the 'twenties could well read like a catalogue of forgotten musicians who were fortunate enough to see their names in lights for a few short weeks before they disappeared as the winds of public taste suddenly changed direction. But I am writing neither an encyclopaedia nor a trade directory. We shall content ourselves with studying the rock-face rather than each grain of sand.

The 'twenties: age of flat-bosomed young ladies posing in aesthetic attitudes and enormous hats; the "flicks" and 2LO; Edith Sitwell's *Façade*, Huxley's cocktail-set novels and music by Satie and Lord Berners; giggling and General Strikes; vo-do-de-o-do and *The Waste Land*; Socialism advancing, Liberalism retreating and nobody caring either way; and jazz.

Not that the post-war generation ever dreamed that jazz music could be upheld as one of the most distinctive characteristics of their decade. By 1921 it was dying. "Jerky tunes and jazz have gone," announced the *Daily Mail*, and a host of similar obituaries reiterated the point. There was some truth in it. Some of the West End restaurants were reverting to sleepy string combinations, claiming that diners were finding that jazz and the digestive process are poor mixers. Second-hand stores and pawn-shops began to fill out with an assortment of discarded novelty percussion instruments, and none of the visiting American groups had the success that had attended the O.D.J.B. The name jazz was beginning to give way to the older and more dignified term "syncopated music", which had the effect of rendering both terms vague to the point of being meaningless. All syncopated music was jazz, in popular estimation, as all jazz was syncopated music. Thus, when Percy Grainger's composition "In a Nutshell" was given its first performance in January 1921, the public were informed by the *Daily Mail* that "The Queen's Hall Orchestra indulged in half an hour of jazz at the Symphony Concert on Saturday. And why shouldn't they, if they like it . . .?"

Many thought that the death-warrant of jazz was signed when, in 1922, a new form of music crossed the Atlantic. Known as the "blues", it had little in common with the Negro folk-blues—Bessie Smith had yet to make her first record—and was defined by the *Dancing Times* as "a use of discords which does not produce an unpleasant effect upon the harmony". But the style never caught on as jazz had done. It degenerated to a dance-step and became a sort of slow foxtrot before being finally swept away by the tidal wave of fanatical enthusiasm which greeted the next importation—"Symphonic Syncopation".

Since before the turn of the century, gramophone recordings of some of the world's most popular singers had been available on either cylinders or discs. When, at the end of the First World War, recording techniques had been sufficiently improved, dance orchestras were invited to make records to be used for instructional purposes, and within a year or two so great was the demand for dance records that the Gramophone Company, then undisputed leader in the field,

imported masters from America and supplemented its home
catalogue by issuing the pressings here. Among them were a batch
made by the Ambassador Orchestra and their popular young leader
Paul Whiteman.

Even before 1920 Whiteman was very nearly a household name in
the States. Serving with the U.S. Navy during the war, he had every
opportunity of perfecting the art of orchestral arranging since he was
appointed leader of a 40-piece orchestra. On demobilisation he
formed an 8-piece combination and put his name before a wider
public by specialising in the fashionable syncopated dance music,
and it was with this group that he made the first of the many dozens
of records which were released in this country. He eschewed the
current "ragtime" and "jazz" labels, describing his music in terms of
"symphonic syncopation", and his new aesthetic fired the imagination
of those who sought to elevate jazz to a pedestal of spick-and-span
respectability. In Britain the ambassador of the Whiteman gospel was
Bert Ralton, who, until his death in a car crash, led the Savoy Havana
Band, which boasted three saxophones, clarinet, French horn, trombone, violin, cello, piano and drums. But even this grandiose array
was put to shame when, in April 1923, the Master himself brought
his orchestra to England. Advertised as a "Jazz Orchestra", Whiteman's new combination consisted of two trumpets (doubling on
flügel-horns), two trombones, two French horns, a flute, a varying
array of saxophones, clarinets and oboes, eight violins, two double-
basses (doubling on tuba), a banjo, a piano and drums.

The music produced by this distinctly un-Dixieland conglomeration
varied from jazz-like syncopated dance material to relatively straight
"interpretations" of popular classics. "He gave us a piece of real jazz",
says one of his hearers, "as it was played before his coming. There
was all the blare and discord and the lack of melody as we used to
know it, and, alas, as we still know it in some places. Then he played
the same tune as he would render it today, and in a moment one

realised what Whiteman means when he talks of 'symphonising syncopation'."[1] But this is nothing to the ecstatic raptures with which he was received by some critics. "Paul Whiteman's musicianship", wrote one, "is equalled only by his showmanship. Both have been matured by him into fine arts. His great, bluff personality fits our idea of the jazz musician completely. At the Savage Club, Whiteman proved to his audience that he was something more than a mere fiddler and conductor of dance tunes. *Delving into the classics, he displayed touches of genuine virtuosity rivalling the greatest of the world's violinists.* . . . [He] came to us with a reputation as a jazz conductor. He will leave us with that reputation considerably enhanced."[2]

One does not have to be a jazz purist to insist that there was just about as much jazz interest in Whiteman's Orchestra[3] as there is today in Jimmy Shand and his Band. Nevertheless, his visit was important in that it served to revive or maintain an interest in jazz music of sorts. Whether or not this little service counterbalances the enormous effect it had in perpetuating and consolidating the man-in-the-street's total lack of comprehension concerning what jazz was and what it was not, is a matter of conjecture. But if he did nothing else, Paul Whiteman ensured that the word "jazz" remained in the English vocabulary.

When he returned to New York, Ralph Hawkes and Arthur Capel organised The London Band, continuing in the apostle's doctrine. Other similar groups sprang up throughout the provinces, and musicians who had long jibbed at associating themselves with the Dixieland or bang-crash Dr. Crock manifestations of jazz enthusiastically joined themselves to the cause of Symphonic Syncopation. Jazz began to be regarded as a living, growing organism; an art-form

[1] *Dancing Times*, May 1923.

[2] *Dancing Times*, May 1923. Italics mine.

[3] i.e. as it was in 1923. Later, Whiteman employed "hot" soloists, among them Bix Beiderbecke.

with a history. It had started life in low quarters in America—some cads actually suggested that niggers had had a hand in it—and had gradually progressed until now, as a people's art, it was ready to march against the staid, stolid "classical music" world and replace it with a syncopated millennium. For years the more solemn musical monthlies and quarterlies had either ignored jazz altogether or predicted its early demise; the tables were now turned, and with a new-found confidence in their art the revolutionary wing began to invade enemy territory. The practice of "jazzing the classics" was encouraged as being in tune with the times. After all, "Franz Schubert used to amuse his friends by putting tissue-paper over a comb and singing the 'Erl King' through it. If Schubert, the greatest of all song-writers, had a right thus to sing his biggest song with muted sounds and exaggerated expression, why not then let us be modest and admit that if the greatest of all song-writers was willing to jazz his greatest song, why should anyone raise his hands at the jazzing of other classics?"[1]

Jack Hylton was perhaps the first to clearly formulate the creed of the progressives. Jazz came, he says, "from the jungle via America. Certainly in its first state it had much crudeness. It sprang upon us with a good deal of noise and discord. That perfect concord of instruments which makes the dance orchestras of today so popular, had not been reached. It could only be reached by much effort, by continual elimination, by a harmonisation combined with a perfection of rhythm. If its origin lies in the beat of the tom-tom in the jungle, remember also that the stars began as clouds of floating dust in the heavens, and that the orchid springs from an ugly brown seed.

". . . As jazz evolved and began to call harmony to its assistance— for it could not have lived long without it—syncopated music became a combination of these two qualities, rhythm and harmony. Beauty began to creep into the new form of music, so that today we have a form of musical expression which can please both those who love

[1] *Melody Maker*, July 1926.

harmony but care not for mere rhythm, and those who love rhythm but care not for harmony. Syncopation is the compromise between rhythm and harmony, between savagery and intellectualism. It is the music of the normal human being, and because of this it will live —progressively of course and gradually evolving into new forms— but it will live."[1]

This is a far, far cry from the jazz that was cradled in Storyville, New Orleans; and an almost equally far cry from its first remove, the music of the Original Dixieland Jazz Band. Where does the lusty music of a New Orleans parade fit into Jack Hylton's scheme of things?

It was some time before the turn of the tide, although the seeds of the turning-point were planted long before they actually flowered. In 1923 Paul Specht settled in Britain for a time, opened with his own orchestra at Lyons' Corner House, Coventry Street, and did much by way of critical comment to preserve a little understanding of jazz. Then in 1925 London received the Mound City Blue Blowers, a group of young men from Chicago who had learnt their jazz from no less a set of masters than the members of King Oliver's Creole Jazz Band—which latter group was one day to be recognised as perhaps the finest ever. The Blue Blowers were led by Red McKenzie, who, fired with a desire to create jazz after the manner of the New Orleans men in Chicago, and yet unable to play an instrument, had taken up the nursery instrument of comb and tissue-paper, the playing of which he developed to a fine art. He had little difficulty in gathering around his imitation-cornet lead such fellow-enthusiasts as guitarist Eddie Lang (at that time working with a "sweet" orchestra at the Knicker-bocker Hotel, where no one dreamed that he was to become one of the world's finest white jazzmen on his chosen instrument), banjoist Jack Bland, Dick Slevin on kazoo (an instrument functioning on the comb-and-paper principle) and Gordon Means on a suitcase, which he "played" by placing wrapping-paper between the straps, striking

[1] Quoted from the first issue of the *Melody Maker*, January 1926.

47

this with shoe brushes and supplying the bass beat by the simple expedient of kicking the suitcase. Variety was added by their humming into jugs, tins, bottles and anything else handy.

This sounds like the "comic hat" band with a vengeance. In fact, their music was finer and nearer the essence of jazz than that supplied by any group since the departure of the Original Dixielanders. But London was not wildly enthusiastic; perhaps she would have preferred the Blue Blowers' line-up of a few years later, when Eddie Condon, Glenn Miller, Jack Teagarden and "Pee Wee" Russell were playing with them. Nevertheless, they left their mark on the provinces, and particularly on the industrial centres in the Midlands and Lancashire, where amateur bands with a kazoo-and-drums instrumentation organised themselves into leagues, competed for cups and became accepted as necessary elements in the fabric of working-class life. But although based on some degree of improvisation and in spite of using the title "Jazz Band", the influence of the Mound City Blue Blowers was no longer of any significance by the time they had reached peak popularity just after the 1926 General Strike.

In 1927 there appeared the first book on jazz to be published in this country. R. W. S. Mendl's *The Appeal of Jazz* was a serious study of the music as it then appeared to an intelligent Englishman, and although it can hardly be claimed that the author had any grounding in the musical background of Negro New Orleans, he certainly seems to have had a deeper insight into the essentials of jazz than those who were promulgating the Whiteman doctrine, and did a great deal in mediating between the "popular" and "classical" camps which were then at daggers drawn.

Much of British jazz he finds trite, commonplace and vulgar; but on the other hand he is aware of an "undercurrent of melancholy or pathos" in the best of it. He brings to notice the element of improvisation which he finds in some bands and likens such a group to "the

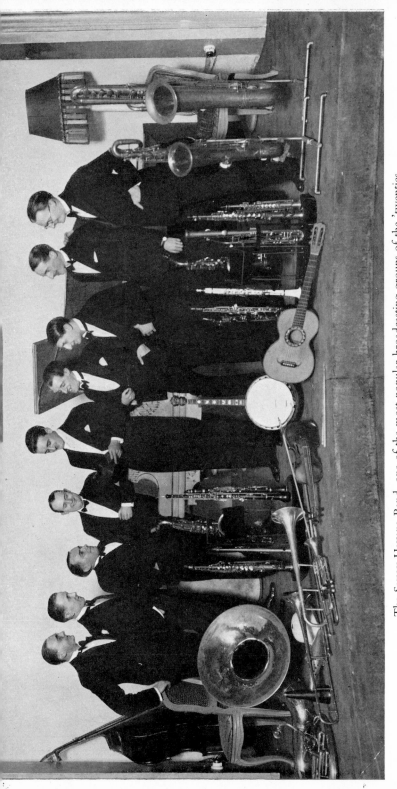

The Savoy Havana Band, one of the most popular broadcasting groups of the 'twenties.

Left to right: Harry Evans (bs), Anthony Thorpe (tb), Dave Thomas (bj), Laurie Huntington (ds), Reg. Batten (Leader & vn), Harry Howard (p), Max Goldberg (tp), Leslie Bates (2nd sax), Van Phillips (1st sax).

Spike Hug
whose rec
ing activ
between
and 1933
volution
British j
He is now
known a
popular w
on "serio
music
opera.

Fred Elizalde, who introduced "hot jazz" as a live commodity in London in

early performers of traditional folk-melodies in that it alters the character of its material entirely". Furthermore, he rebukes the serious-music fraternity for their studied indifference to the existence of a music which "has attracted the white folk of the United States, the masses of the British Isles, the people of practically every country in Europe, of Canada, of Australia, of New Zealand and South America", noting that "in every quarter of the globe where white races dwell, jazz has obtained a footing".

He goes on to analyse in some detail the reasons why jazz continued to attract such an army of haters, classifying their objections into six categories, all of which we would retain today. First he considers those who object to the sensuality of jazz and agrees that "If we find the unrestrained excess of sexual desire or gratification, or some kind of sexual perversion, portrayed in terms of music, then we may reasonably object to it. We may say that this goes too far, that there must be some artistic limit to the frank portrayal of human impulses." But, he continues, "Surely we cannot fairly say this of jazz. Personally I find the element of sex present in a far weaker degree in this music than I do in many waltzes. Numbers of the waltz tunes which have been popular during the last thirty years have been literally steeped in sexual desire of the most voluptuous kind imaginable. A great deal of their popularity must, if we are quite honest with ourselves, be traced to this source. But jazz! Frankly, I rub my eyes at the strange notion that it is remarkably sensual . . . and I believe that most people—music-lovers or others—who asked themselves whether they really considered jazz music to be markedly voluptuous would reply in the negative."

Mendl rebuts the charge that jazz makes too much noise by reference to the music then being composed for the concert-hall. He further invokes the aid of Bach and Beethoven—in particular the latter's Seventh Symphony—in correcting the popular view that jazz lacks subtlety of rhythm, and the classical masters are also called in to defend it from the charge of being "cynically grotesque". "If grotesqueness in music be a sin," he argues, "then woe betide Beethoven for the Trio of the C Minor Symphony, Grieg for 'The Hall of the Mountain King' and César Franck for 'Les Djinns' and 'Le Chausseur Maudit'; let Wagner tremble for his Mime, and Berlioz for his Witches' Sabbath." He might have added a dash of Stravinsky —"Petrouchka" for instance—and the whole Mahler corpus; but he made his point, amply demonstrating that the cynical and grotesque in music are to be found as often in the concert-hall as the dance-hall.

The book finally discusses colour prejudice as a barrier to jazz appreciation, providing a healthy antidote to the silly snobbery which had led even so pro-jazz a magazine as the *Melody Maker* to "demand that the habit of associating our music with the primitive and barbarous Negro derivations shall cease forthwith, in justice to the obvious fact that we have out-grown such comparisons".[1] On the whole, and considering the misconceptions current when it appeared, *The Appeal of Jazz* provided a thoughtful and nicely balanced statement of opinion, heralding the coming revival of interest in true jazz to which our attention must now be turned.

By the middle '20s it was beginning to be recognised that jazz in England was a very different affair from jazz in America. And it was different not as a "progressive improvement" upon the parent product but rather as a progressive deviation. It became increasingly evident, too, that the British public were finding more of interest in the American styles than in those featured by the London Club bands, and only by learning from his American counterpart could the British musician hope to retain his following. "The new ideas which American bands are continually introducing seem to maintain and stimulate the general interest in, and desire for, this type of music among the lay

[1] Editorial, June 1926.

masses, upon which interest the British musician is absolutely dependent for his present livelihood. At the moment he compares with the milliner's copyist who some day, but not just yet, will become the designer."[1]

Things came to a head when, in 1926, Paul Whiteman made a second visit to Britain with a 27-piece orchestra. The whole country was given the opportunity of hearing him as he performed in London, Liverpool, Sheffield, Birmingham, Manchester, Blackpool, Glasgow, Edinburgh, Newcastle, Bradford, Leicester and Brighton. The symphonic-syncopating fraternity—who for three or four years had ruled the roost—were amazed and aggrieved to find that the daily press were not disposed to repeat their rave-notices of three years earlier. Instead, they referred to "shattering explosions", "inexorable rhythms", "jingly tunes", "grotesque forms" and the like. This for the "King of Jazz"! "Jazz music has its enemies," retorted the *Melody Maker* grimly, "and they will do all in their power to oust this new form of music." But it was the public who were right; symphonic jazz was a dying music.

Its successor was a small-group style featuring the improvised solo. To distinguish it from the Whiteman school it was christened "Hot Jazz", and a steadily increasing stream of records from America served only to create an ever-widening demand. Such groups as the Goofus Five, the Cotton Pickers and the Memphis Five; such names as Miff Mole and Red Nicholls; these began to be bandied about in British jazz circles, and their influence was enormous. Articles on "How to play 'Hot' trumpet", "How to play 'Hot' trombone"— even "How to play 'Hot' cymbals" appeared in the pages of the *Melody Maker*, which, after a change in ownership, embarked on a policy of whole-hearted support for the new style. "His Master's Voice", "Parlophone", "Brunswick-Cliftophone" and other labels were continuing to pour out American records, and although the

[1] *Melody Maker*, March 1926.

most enthusiasm centred around the Nicholls-Mole school, such names as Johnny Dodds (with his Black Bottom Stompers) and Clarence Williams (with his Bottomland Orchestra) were also receiving a hearing. During 1927 Fletcher Henderson, Duke Ellington and "Jelly Roll" Morton also made their bow before the British public; Fletcher Henderson's first batch of records were described as "far better than those we are used to hearing from the average nigger band", and Ellington was introduced as the leader of "a coloured unit in which the expected faults of coon bands—a noticeable crudeness and somewhat poor tone—are by no means so apparent as usual". Only the Morton Red Hot Peppers were castigated without qualification, being described as "hopelessly old-fashioned in style, even if the musicians can play their instruments". But the general tenor of critical comment was none the less in favour of "hot" as opposed to "symphonic".

New movements need a spearhead, and a champion of "hot" style was forthcoming in Spanish-born pianist and all-round musician Fred Elizalde, who came to Britain in 1926 in order to be with his brother, Manuel "Liz" Elizalde, then a Cambridge undergraduate. Although not himself a student at the University, Fred was soon the acknowledged leader of the Manuel set, and in 1927 he demonstrated his enthusiasm for jazz by organising an undergraduate band known as the Quinquaginta Ramblers. By the summer he had the band recording for Brunswick, but this was by no means the fulfilment of his ambitions and within two or three months he had collected together the finest "hot" musicians in the country—Jack Miranda on clarinet and alto, Jack Jackson and Norman Payne on trumpets, Joe Crossman on tenor, Perley Breed on alto, Dick Escott on tuba, Joe Branelly on banjo and Max Bacon on drums—cutting the first jazz records of genuine worth to be made entirely by a British unit.

As luck would have it, the management of London's Savoy Hotel were on the lookout for a first-class band leader, and the enthusiastic director of the Brunswick company, Count Anthony di Bosdari, suggested the name of Fred Elizalde. January 1st, 1928, found him in his new appointment as leader of the finest dance band of any jazz interest in the country. But still perfectionist Elizalde was not entirely satisfied, and within a few weeks he had managed to entice a galaxy of American stars to cross the Atlantic and work with him. Out of the blue, as it seemed, the British jazz fan found himself confronted with such men as Adrian Rollini (who had led an all-star group in New York, consisting of Joe Venuti, Eddie Lang, Bix Beiderbecke and Frank Signorelli), Bobby Davis (who was famous as leading alto on the Goofus Five and Goofus Washboards records), Chelsea Quealey (who was billed as being "on a par with Red Nicholls and Bix Beiderbecke"), Fud Livingstone and Max Farley. The recordings made by Brunswick of this Anglo-American group were undoubtedly the finest made in England during that decade.

Elizalde also proved himself an interesting soloist, but he was as prolific with the pen as he was at the keyboard. Through the pages of the *Melody Maker* he was the first to introduce to British fans the names of many American musicians who have since risen to the tops of their respective ladders, or have become romantic legends. Thus *Bix Bidlebeck* (Elizalde's first attempt at the spelling) was announced as "the greatest trumpet player of all time"—so much ahead of his time, says Elizalde, that he was actually playing "hot" music five years before anyone else cottoned on to it! *Louis Armstrong* also made his bow, bracketed with rival Ted Schilling: "We foresee the brightest of futures for Schilling especially. In fact we expect him to be the best trumpet player across the Atlantic before a couple of years are gone. . . . [He has] absolute originality of style and phrasing and hardly ever does the same things, or anything like them, twice in the same tune." Of Armstrong, to whom the above words would perfectly apply, we are advised that his "great feature is, in addition to great technical ability, that there is such heart in his playing". *Fletcher*

Henderson has "far and away the best coloured dance orchestra playing today"; *Bennie Goodman* is praised as "a master saxophone player whose name has not yet reached this side of the world, but whose playing entitles him to everyone's admiration"; *Jimmy Dorsey* is described as "the best saxophone player who ever played dance music"; and Miff Mole is ceremoniously enthroned as "the best trombone player that ever attempted to play a 'hot' chorus".

It is as easy to sneer at these critical snippets today as it is to disregard Fred Elizalde for not playing like Bunk Johnson. Nevertheless, it remains almost certain that, without the visiting Spaniard, "hot" style would have languished for lack of a champion. As it was, it became a commercial proposition. Jack Hylton engaged "hot" trumpeter Jack Jackson, and the Ambrose and Lew Stone big bands also found a place for the "hot" soloist. Elizalde deserves more of the credit for creating and channelling public demand than most of us realise.

In 1930 he returned to his homeland to continue more serious musical studies under Manuel de Falla, subsequently devoting himself to the composition of an opera on the life of Gauguin, various symphonic poems and piano and violin concertos. Between attacks of creative inspiration he fought for the Caudillo with all the energy that he had previously put into fighting for "hot" music. He is now head of the Manila Broadcasting Station, his triumphs at the Savoy nearly three decades behind him.

And his mantle fell on a young string bass player, an Irishman by the name of Patrick Cairns Hughes.

Chapter 5

REVIVAL AND DECLINE

Spike Hughes took over from Fred Elizalde as the first name in British jazz, and as a prominent jazz critic. In 1933 he gave up his recording activities and concentrated on writing. Louis Armstrong and Duke Ellington visited the country and greatly extended the jazz public. Constant Lambert's book Music Ho! *brought jazz to the notice of the serious music-lover.*

The term "swing" began to replace "hot jazz" and was in turn taken over by the commercial semi-jazz big bands.

THE fourth decade of the century found jazz in Great Britain to be something more than the sickly child so superciliously denigrated by many critics of today who find it easy to be wise after the event. A "hot jazz" public was now in being, its members found in every strata of English life, from the duchess to the dole-drawer. Second-hand record shops were being systematically combed, and old, dusty, chipped discs made a decade earlier by the Original Dixieland Jazz Band fetched three times as much as mint Ellington. The amateur "Dixie" bands that were still entertaining friends and neighbours with a music not altogether different from that introduced by Nick La Rocca and Larry Shields now began to find themselves not quite the insignificant wing of jazz musicians that they had long grown accustomed to be.

Nevertheless, it was uphill work. The old "nice-and-tidy, sweet-and-dignified" school of jazz still had its legion of followers, though by now most of them had thrown overboard the "jazz" label as being unworthy of the music it claimed to cover, scolding Columbia for advertising a record as "real jazz" and "hastening to enlighten them by saying that it signifies everything that is bad and everything that is old-fashioned. It is a word of sarcasm." Thus, even in 1930, the convention that Negro bands were either crude or funny, or both, but never of real value, was by no means dead, and we find in April of that year a review of Duke Ellington's "Hot and Bothered" in which the orchestration is described as "a masterpiece of instrumental humour", parts of which were "absolutely shriekingly funny". It is difficult not to be reminded of Jack Point's wry observation that "an accepted wit has only to say 'Pass the mustard' and they roar their ribs out".

The old attitude, then, was dying hard; but it was nevertheless dying. When, on November 30th, 1929, Christopher Stone of the *Gramophone* broadcast an illustrated talk on Negro music with the object of presenting "the real thing in place of the imitations that we have come to accept", using such examples as "Ain't Misbehavin'" and "Basin Street Blues" as performed by the Louis Armstrong Hot Five, "Fifty-Seven Variations" played by Earl Hines and "Am I Blue" as sung by Ethel Waters, the B.B.C. was flooded with hundreds of wildly enthusiastic letters. The great split in the jazz public—the split that separated those who wanted their music to be "nice" from those who wanted it "hot"—was to grow until each party was virtually divorced from the other. The pro-nice set found their rallying point in the film "King of Jazz", featuring the old idol, Paul Whiteman. Opening in London in June 1930, it was described on the hoardings as "undeniably the most colossal, lavish and gorgeous effort ever put on the screen". But although it served to pull together those who persisted in seeing symphonic syncopation as the music of the future, it failed to counteract the even stronger pull exerted by a twenty-one-year-old newcomer to the "hot" ranks who was to dominate the British recording scene for three years and lead the tastes of his generation for very nearly ten.

Patrick "Spike" Hughes was born on October 19th, 1908. That he was to develop a keen ear for music was more or less a foregone conclusion, his mother having had some success as a concert pianist and his father as a music critic. His musical education began when he was six with a study of the violin, but this proved to be a false start. On completion of his general education he travelled extensively on the Continent, studying conducting in Berlin and trying his hand at his father's game of musical journalism. When only sixteen his interest in jazz music led him to form his own collection of the Red Nicholls Five Pennies recordings, and he spent the next five years in gradually absorbing something of the character of "hot" music. In the spring of 1930 he gathered to himself a handful of like-minded enthusiasts, most of them members of the well-known big bands where opportunities for uncompromisingly "hot" phrasing and free and easy improvisation were limited. He persuaded Decca to devote a session to them and issued his first titles under the exotic name of Spike Hughes and his Decca-dents.

His first arrangements followed the current Red Nicholls-Miff Mole pattern. In the three years subsequent to May 1930 a steady stream of them invaded the record-market, and it became apparent that Hughes was Elizalde's successor. His prestige was further enhanced when, later in the same year, the Ted Lewis Orchestra visited Britain and Hughes managed to secure their alto-man, twenty-six-year-old Jimmy Dorsey, for a recording session with drummer Bill Harty, guitarist Alan Ferguson and Claude Ivy on piano. With the resulting issues, Hughes became a household word wherever British jazz was thought to be of any consequence, and the *Melody Maker* spared no pains to espouse his cause, describing him as "the most interesting personality that the English fold of dance musicians has ever produced", "this modernistic demi-god of the bass-viol" and "a hundred per cent. genius with the rhythmic ability of an Armstrong and the musical assurance of a Stravinsky".

If we cannot take this seriously today, the fact remains that he was head and shoulders above his contemporaries as a composer and arranger. His best originals, "Sirocco", "Six Bells Stampede", "Nocturne", "Elegy" and "A Harlem Symphony", are the first British jazz compositions of real intrinsic (as distinct from historical) value, and the two sides comprising the "Symphony" stand unsurpassed, even today, in the field of British arranging; and this in spite of the fact that they were composed, scored, rehearsed and recorded within the space of thirty-six hours. The dedication of this piece—"in admiration to Duke Ellington"—is significant. The Duke's influence had replaced that of Red Nicholls, apparent in the early "Decca-dents" sides, and Hughes was now creating an impressionistic mood-music of considerable power.

The Dance Orchestra, as Hughes—or Decca—now preferred to call it, remained a recording unit only. Norman Payne, Arthur Niblo and Leslie Thompson took on most of the trumpet work on the earlier sessions, with Jimmy Macaffer, Billy Higgs and Chick Smith taking their places on the later sides; Lew Davis and Bill Mulraney looked after the trombones, and the sax family were operated by Harry Hines, Buddy Featherstonehaugh and Billy Amstell; and again, to support the rhythm laid down by "Spike's" own bass, Alan Ferguson played guitar, Ronnie Gubertini and Bill Harty alternated at the drums, and Eddie Carroll, later succeeded by Billy Mason, warmed the piano-stool. Like Elizalde again, Hughes was as prolific and proficient with the pen as he was with four strings, and the articles and reviews published in the *Melody Maker*, both under his own name and his pseudonym "Mike", did much throughout the '30s to maintain a healthy attitude towards "hot" music.

Writing in *Swing Music* in 1935, he tells us something of his method of composition: "In the beginning there is always The Title. With the exception of 'Elegy' (1932) and 'Nocturne' (1933) ... every piece I ever wrote for the band was first inspired by a title. Even in the days when I wrote 'straight' music, it was always 'about' something."

This somewhat slap-happy method is perhaps best exemplified in "Sirocco", which takes its name from the south wind which sweeps over the Mediterranean from the Sahara, hot and dry, irritating and depressing. The composition invokes such a mood to a quite extraordinary degree; it is a subtle, disturbing piece—one that, once put on the turntable, insists on returning there again and again.

In 1933 Hughes visited New York and spent a great deal of time in Harlem playing his own and traditional compositions with some of his idols. When he returned to England, he could no longer be persuaded to return to the recording studios; the music of his old British colleagues had lost its appeal, as far as he was concerned. "When I went to America," he explains, "I had the pick of Harlem's players for recording. Any band in Europe would have been an anticlimax thereafter. More than that: no sane man tries to pick up the threads of a love affair once they are broken. Those American recordings were like that. They gave me all I ever wanted in jazz: to have a Negro orchestra play my music. After that there was nothing."

But there was more to it than that: "People began to take seriously something that I and my collaborators had enjoyed as a diversion. . . . People began to give recitals of our records, discuss classical influences, tendencies and the rest. Before long we were Art. . . . But because jazz was nothing more than an afternoon's walk, I began to get very suspicious of people who tried to magnify its importance. I found myself saying: 'Well, if that's the sort of person who buys my records I shan't make any more.' " [1]

There was certainly no financial inducement for him to continue doing so. The full fee for each session had never exceeded £45, which had to cover all remuneration and expenses. Today, Patrick Hughes is a popular writer on concert music and opera; he *has* in fact picked up the threads of a love affair, and that his first. But he will not be forgotten in the world of British jazz.

[1] *Rhythm*, April 1937.

In 1932 the "Back to New Orleans!" cry made its debut in England. Although the Crescent City was still by no means acknowledged as the cradle of jazz, the Dixieland style as exemplified by the venerated Original Dixieland Jazz Band had an ever-increasing number of adherents, and although the vast majority of these never dreamed that any real revival in the fortunes of their music could ever come about, there was the occasional odd man out, the man of imagination, who lived for the day when old-time jazz would once again come into its own. One such was Derrick Turner, who, although no brilliant musician himself, had a tremendous enthusiasm for genuine, down-to-earth jazz. He managed to obtain a one-night booking at the Café de Paris, where he presented his New Dixieland Band, consisting of Alf Noakes on trumpet, Sid Lenton on clarinet, the indispensable Lew Davis (who had never forgotten that "Joy Bells" night) on trombone and Dave Frost on piano, with drummer Harry Bentley responsible for both the beat and the vocals. The one-night stand proved utterly insufficient to cater for the sudden interest aroused, and the Café management promptly offered Turner a regular contract. All but pianist Frost had commitments elsewhere, but the determined Mr. Turner organised a frantic search and managed to uncover drummer-vocalist Frank Morgan to provide with Dave Frost the necessary beat, and front-line men Harry Owen on trumpet, Sid Milward on clarinet and Harry Collins on trombone. In the succeeding weeks they attracted a great deal of attention; but Britain was not yet ripe for a consummate revelation of jazz à la Storyville—even if the New Dixielanders had been able to supply it—and when the public found the novelty wearing a little thin, the Café de Paris were obliged to return to their policy of satisfying the old tastes. The five musicians returned to their Jekyll and Hyde careers, pleasing the public in working hours and getting down to the real jazz when the rare opportunity arose; and Derrick Turner returned to his records.

A little later in the same year British jazz received its biggest inspiration and incentive to improvement when Louis Armstrong came to London. Since his name had first become familiar to jazz enthusiasts in 1927, Armstrong had rapidly become a living legend. The Fletcher Henderson recordings in which he featured, together with his own Hot Five discs, had spread his fame into every little corner of the country. Two overwhelmingly successful weeks at the Palladium were followed by visits to Nottingham and Glasgow, where his welcome was no less warm and his music no less hot. Backed as he was by a small group of coloured musicians imported from Paris, the quality of the music produced by the group was not to be compared with that produced by the Hot Five, but Armstrong was capable then, as he is today, of producing some of his best work in some of the worst circumstances. He gives the impression that he is perfectly capable of producing great jazz with the backing of nothing more than a clacking metronome.

His technical virtuosity and his rich, red-hot personality gained many new converts to jazz music. Every one of his concerts was given national press coverage. When, a few months after his return to America, the *Daily Express* headlined on its front page an account of his death, a flood of tearful and hysterical letters arriving at the *Melody Maker* offices bore tribute to the affection in which he was held in Britain. It transpired that he had been nipped in the leg by a rather depressed dog and rumour had magnified the event out of all proportion.

"Fats" Waller followed Armstrong to Britain in September of the same year, consolidating and building up a large following for the happy, exuberant brand of piano-and-vocal jazz which has always been associated with him. "Hot" jazz had come into its own; "symphonic syncopation", after a few convulsive gasps, slid gently below the ruffled surface, where, we trust, it now rests in peace.

By this time it was recognised that a "hot" chorus must give the *impression* of having been delivered extempore—"sent before its time into this breathing world, scarce half made up"—but there were few musicians who failed to work out beforehand every little detail of their dozen-or-so bars in the limelight. The *Melody Maker* published each month a selection of ready-made choruses, sometimes as many as seven or eight pages of them, which were faithfully adhered to by dozens of musicians up and down the country. The Armstrong and Waller visits did something to weaken this state of affairs, and the flood of records that continued to flow in from the States, particularly those on Parlophone's "New Rhythm Style" series, continued to point the way to a freer, less inhibited mode of playing. "Muggsy" Spanier had joined Benny Goodman as the recognised leader—in so far as Britain was concerned—of the Chicago set. Don Redman, Luis Russell, Chick Webb and the Dorsey brothers were, after Armstrong, the best-selling artists. The Fletcher Henderson band, whose popularity had waned a little since the late '20s' jazz enlightenment, was now making a spectacular come-back and ranked second only to Ellington. "Both individually and collectively," advised the *Melody Maker* (April 1932), "it is almost without a peer among Negro bands, which means necessarily that no white band can touch it." The enlightenment was growing.

On May 13th, 1932, the B.B.C. put over a thirty-five-minute programme devoted entirely to Duke Ellington. The reception it was accorded indicated what had long been apparent from the record-sales figures, namely that the Duke had a following in every section of the jazz and dance music publics. Early the following year Ellington sent representatives to Britain for the purpose of gauging public demand for his music, and in June 1933 the finest large combination in jazz history was playing in London. In the succeeding months jazz enthusiasts in the provinces converged on Brighton, Hastings, Bolton, Blackpool, Harrogate, Bridlington and Glasgow, where the orchestra filled the largest halls night after night. "The Mooche", "Mood Indigo", "Black and Tan Fantasy", along with a dozen other titles subsequently to become classics of jazz, fell on British ears for the first time.

Britain was fortunate in hearing Ellington in the flesh at a time when he himself was at his creative peak and his band the finest that he was ever able to muster. Barney Bigard, Johnny Hodges, Harry Carney and Otto Hardwicke proved an unrivalled saxophone-and-clarinet quartet; Arty Whetsol, Charlie "Cootie" Williams and Fred Jenkins assumed the responsibility for the trumpet work; Laurence Brown, Juan Tizol and Joe Nanton handled the trombones; rhythmic backing was provided by Bill Braud on bass, Fred Guy on banjo, Sonny Greer on drums—also taking a large share of the vocals; and, of course, Ellington himself presiding at the piano. Within a few years many of these names were to be numbered among the brightest in the jazz firmament.

But the British enthusiast was not allowed to concentrate all his attention on Ellington, for within a month of the Duke's opening in London, Louis Armstrong was back on a return visit. Again using a pick-up group of coloured musicians recruited from the Paris cafés, he set out to repeat his success of the previous year. Hardly had he set foot on British soil, however, when he quarrelled with his manager, John Collins. Their long-standing partnership, both artistically and financially an outstanding success, was abruptly severed, and Jack Hylton took over the task of managing young Louis' business affairs. On top of this misfortune, Armstrong started his tour badly by totally underestimating the demands of his audience, which was composed, to a large extent, of the more serious section of the jazz-consuming public, still very much under the influence of their recent contact with Ellington. His superabundance of showmanship and instrumental cleverness disappointed and disturbed them. "He seems to have come to the conclusion", mourned one critic, "that a variety artist's only mission in life is to be sensational, to pander to the baser emotions, to sacrifice all art to crude showmanship."[1]

But fortunately this was not the case, and once he had correctly fathomed the difference in approach between his American and British followers, Armstrong was again able to bring to the lips of his critics all the old, choice superlatives. This was the first but by no means the last occasion at which it seemed apparent that the British enthusiast was beginning to overtake his American counterpart in recognition and appreciation of the genuine jazz spirit as distinct from the diluted product turned out, as it were, on the factory belt.

When Armstrong had been here for ten months, it was announced that Coleman Hawkins, star of the Fletcher Henderson combination, was to join him in London for the last few weeks prior to his return to the States. Hawkins arrived, and arrangements were completed for the first-night double presentation. Then Armstrong dramatically pulled out. Nothing that either Hylton or the concert promoters could say would persuade him to change his mind. Hawkins was presented alone, fronting his own pick-up group, and London was deprived of the only opportunity it ever had of hearing the two musicians in concert. In spite of his "temperamental prima-donna" action, Armstrong's popularity continued to rise. His older records[2] became collectors' items, and each of his new issues was acknowledged better than the last. His fame as a vocalist, featuring his meaningless, "scat" singing, rivalled his renown as the world's leading jazz trumpeter, and, above all, his influence extended to almost every front-line man in a British band, from the Nat Gonellas who faithfully

---

[1] *Melody Maker*, August 5th, 1933.

[2] Those dating as far back as his Fletcher Henderson days. The King Oliver and Bessie Smith discs on which he featured were not yet thoroughly explored. Leonard Feather, in preparing an Armstrong discography in 1934, dismisses these with the comment that "there were dozens of titles, all very much the same, and hardly worth listing in full".

imitated his every nuance of phrasing, to the trombone, clarinet and saxophone men who attempted to transfer some of the vigour and heat of Armstrong's horn to their own adopted instruments.

1934 saw Joe Venuti at the London Palladium, a Bessie Smith issue from Parlophone (the first authentic blues to be issued by a British company), the return of Armstrong to the States in a blaze of glory, and a rapid increase in the number of "Hot-Record Circles" flourishing up and down the country. It also saw the publication of Constant Lambert's historic book *Music Ho!*

Although on the Continent a great number of composers of "serious" music had attempted to make use of a jazz idiom in their compositions, following in the wake of America's George Gershwin, British composers had for the most part held aloof from what they believed would prove to be a short-lived fashion, and with the exception of William Walton, who had cocked a snook at the dance music of his day in the 1923 *Façade*, and who had made use of pseudo-jazz phrases and syncopation in his late "Portsmouth Point" overture, jazz music might as well have been non-existent for our musical intelligentsia. Lambert was an original and provocative thinker in matters musical, and he was deeply disturbed at the ever-widening gulf separating the composer of art music from the purveyor of music for entertainment. In *Music Ho!* he attempted to put jazz into perspective as an important element in twentieth-century music, and in doing so he brought it to the attention of a host of readers who would otherwise have considered it quite unworthy of serious thought. He had no sympathy with either the blind jazz haters—"the crusty old colonels, the choleric judges and beer-sodden columnists murmuring 'swamp stuff', 'jungle rhythms', 'Negro decadence' whenever they hear the innocent and anodyne strains of the average English jazz band"—or with the fanatical purist who is "only too eager to point out that the Negroes are the only begetters of a movement that has admittedly swept all over the world", and whose "hysterical enthusiasm" and "sentimental effusions must be so embarrassing to the intelligent Negro himself". Instead he pursued a middle-of-the-road course, insisting that jazz *is* to be taken seriously, if not solemnly. Its value, he believed, lay in the fact that it was "the first dance music to bridge the gap between highbrow and lowbrow successfully. The valse has received august patronage from Beethoven onwards, it is true, but the valses of the nineteenth-century composers are either definite examples of unbending or definite examples of sophistication —sometimes both. Chabrier's 'Fête Polonaise' has an harmonic and orchestral elaboration far beyond anything imagined by the popular valse writers of his time, but the modern highbrow composer who writes a fox-trot can hardly hope to go one better than Duke Ellington, if indeed he can be considered as being in the same class at all."

Unfortunately Lambert shared R. W. S. Mendl's incapacity—it was of course a general incapacity—to distinguish accurately between jazz-proper and jazz-paste. This comes out in his strictures on "jazz songs" and in such dogmatic assertions as that "the importance of the Jewish element in jazz cannot be too strongly emphasised, and . . . at least ninety per cent of jazz tunes are written by Jews". But the shortcomings of the book are far outweighed by its shrewd common sense, and, as we have noticed, it served to introduce jazz to a new and valuable public.

The music was reaching high places.

The term "Hot Jazz" had first been used in connection with the American small groups whose records first appeared in 1926, and it came into being in order that there might be a clear-cut distinction between jazz with roots in improvisation and the arid desert of symphonic syncopation. When, during the early '30s, "hot" music became a popular attraction, the big bands in the public eye began, as we have seen, to feature "hot" soloists. The orchestras led by such men as Bert Ambrose, Lew Stone, Roy Fox and Ray Noble all contained some genuine jazz interest, centering on their soloists; but as the "hot" style thus percolated into every corner of British dance music, the reasons for coining the term were forgotten, and by 1935 it was virtually meaningless—so much so that the B.B.C. actually forbade its use on the grounds that it served no useful purpose.

Nevertheless, it was no less necessary in the eyes of the discerning enthusiast to differentiate between the genuine jazz of the smaller groups and the half-jazz style of the big bands than it had been in the first hey-day of the Five Pennies and the Blue Four. The term "Hot Jazz" was thus superseded by "Swing".

Of its actual origin little is known with real certainty. Douglas Enefer, in the *Daily Dispatch Jazz Book*, passes all the credit to Benny Goodman: "He didn't invent the word. He gave it a new meaning. Until then, musicians who had wanted to describe hard-punching jazz used phrases like: 'Swing it there!' They hadn't got around to changing the verb into a noun. Benny made the change, and started something like a revolution." On the other hand, Leonard Feather believes that the term originated with Ellington's 1932 recording of "It Don't Mean a Thing if it Ain't Got That Swing". Whatever truth we feel able to attach to either of these hypotheses, it must be remembered that, in one form or another, the word "swing" was being used long before it acquired the capital S; it is known to have been used in connection with the syncopated dance music of the First World War, and the waltz preceding that.

"The phrase 'Hot Jazz' has had a derogatory effect on our subject in the past year or two," wrote one correspondent in the *Melody Maker*.[1] "We have, first of all, 'Jazz', a neologism coming from an unknown source, and interpreted as loud, vulgar, harsh, etc. Then next the adjective 'Hot'. Heat is naturally associated with friction and

[1] October 5th, 1935.

speed so that this lends further colour to the meaning of jazz as loud and quick, unharmonious and cacophonous. Other names I recall are Rhythm-Style, Blue Rhythm, Modern Rhythm-Style and finally Modern Rhythm. . . . We are now using the word 'Swing' and I consider it perfectly interprets the feelings expressed by our subject."

But "Swing" was no magic password, and it was not long before it was as vague and meaningless as "Hot Jazz" had become. For one thing, the word appears to have had a different meaning for different people. One group of enthusiasts, under the banner of Leonard Hibb's short-lived publication *Swing Music*, tried to restrict it to a particular style of jazz, and when it was discovered that Ellington's individuality kept him apart from the elect, that was hard luck on Ellington. Another wing of opinion used the term exclusively in its rhythmical sense, and yet another applied it to dance bands in general. Before long the word was nothing more significant than a synonym of "good" or "what I like", and as soon as this became apparent the growing army of commercial band leaders adopted it and it was thus applied to the very music to which it had been designed to give the cold shoulder.

And, of course, once the commercial bands had adopted the word the true jazz enthusiast was quick to disown it. Thus the large dance orchestras became identified as the "Swing Bands", and when, ten years later, reaction set in against the whole conception of jazz current in the late '30s, the term became one of contempt—a synonym not of "good" but of "commercial". Now that this reaction has moderated and the old "Swing Bands" are no longer cursed as vehemently as they were in the early crusading days of the New Orleans revival, the word has once again become part of our vocabulary.

By the mid-'30s, then, jazz of one sort or another had become sufficiently remunerative financially for the band leaders and promoters to start abandoning the old economically small groups for the large, lush combinations purveying loud, lush music. But the small groups did not die out altogether, nor did their purer strain of jazz. In 1935 Leonard Feather wrote a series on "Evergreens of Jazz" for the *Melody Maker* in which he brought to the fore such figures as Clarence Williams, King Oliver, W. C. Handy and the forgotten "Jelly Roll" Morton. A Rhythm Clubs' Federation was founded and received excellent support after the dispelling of initial doubts regarding the autonomy of local branches. In February 1936 Brunswick issued an album devoted to Oliver's Creole Jazz Band. Ethel Waters was increasingly well represented in the catalogues, and only two years were to pass before a Bessie Smith album was on the market. Debate and discussion on New Orleans jazz as distinct from the Chicago and New York schools was by no means as impossible as some have supposed, and the recordings made by Wingy Manone's New Orleans Rhythm Kings, formed for the express purpose of "reviving the Dixieland tradition in all its glories", were being bought by many who jibbed at the old masters themselves. Hugues Panassié's book, *Le Jazz Hot*, was published in an English translation in 1936. And Armstrong continued to dominate the record market.

In 1935 Britain's Musicians' Union quarrelled with the American Federation of Musicians, and for the next twenty years the constant visits paid by American bands during the '20s and early '30s were virtually impossible. Live jazz music in Britain seemed for a while to be a thing of the past, making only spasmodic reappearances. Nat Gonella, an avowed imitator of Armstrong, did a little work with small groups of his own, in addition to playing with such bands as those led by Lew Stone and Roy Fox; and trombonist George Chisholm, also an habitué of the big band, made his bow and established himself as perhaps the finest player of his instrument in the country.

In 1936 the B.B.C. Dance Orchestra secured the services of Benny Carter, leader of one of the most successful swing bands in the States, as resident arranger. "When you made Benny Carter's band in those days the stamp was on you. Then you could go with Chick Webb or Fletcher Henderson or any other of the bands. Every time Benny got a band together all the cats would want to know who was in his band because if you could make Benny Carter's band, that was it."[1] With such a reputation it was natural that, during his stay in England, he should become the centre of the country's jazz interest. His flair for recognising and developing talent latent in others was no less evident in London than it had been in New York, and he it was who showed Britain what an asset she possessed in George Chisholm, who, with his Jive Five (Chisholm, trombone; Tommy McQuater, trumpet; Benny Winestone, clarinet and tenor saxophone; Eddie Macaulay, piano; Tiny Winters, bass; Dudley Barber, drums), produced a music which was head and shoulders above the output of his contemporaries.

It is often assumed, quite wrongly, that the decline in the quality of both British and American jazz in the late '30s and during the war years was not apparent to critics, the musicians or the public until better times began to put things in perspective in the late '40s. But, on the contrary, more than one voice was raised in protest. "Spike" Hughes made use of his opportunity as record-reviewer "Mike" of the *Melody Maker* to deplore the current decline of the old fun-and-games spirit, and eventually, after finding himself week after week unable to utter a single word of praise for anyone other than "Fats" Waller, he retired from the field in disgust. Critic "Disc-course" of *Rhythm* complained bitterly that "The public is allowed to call the tune so loudly that there are only a few examples today of the original spirit of jazz music, that of a few enthusiasts gathered together for the purpose of playing in a way that not only gave them some spiritual

[1] Danny Barker in *Hear Me Talkin' To Ya*, edited by Nat Shapiro and Nat Hentoff.

satisfaction, but which they also believed to be the only worth-while way of playing."[1]

French critic Hugues Panassié put it into words that might well be given some prominence today: "There is a decline fundamentally due to one fact; losing some of their spontaneity, many musicians have tried to make more 'clever' music, and, committing always the error of deferring to the legitimate music standard, they wanted jazz to become more composed and refined, which was obtained at the expense of sincerity and swing. On the other hand, the effort put into instrumental technique grew to a great extent, spoiling the inspiration of the solos."[2]

If jazz was sick, its sickness was not altogether without virtue. Without the lean years it may well have fallen prey to that most fatal of all diseases, complacency. As it was, the seeds sown in discontent did eventually bear fruit; a little wind was to set the dying embers ablaze again.

[1] May 1938.   [2] *Rhythm*, May 1938.

Chapter 6

THE SWING OF THE PENDULUM

By the late 'thirties and early 'forties a movement to reinstate the old-time jazz of New Orleans began to make headway in America. George Webb's Dixie-landers brought it to a head in Britain when they broad-cast and recorded in 1945. From the Dixielanders sprang the first Lyttelton band, and this, with Graeme Bell's visiting Australian Jazz Band, pursued a policy of "traditional jazz for dancing".

Within a few years, Ken Colyer was pioneering the field of archaic New Orleans jazz, whilst other traditional musicians explored a loose "main-stream" style.

So much has been written about the New Orleans Revival that it has become increasingly difficult to obtain, from the documentary evidence—much of it vague and self-contradictory—a very clear picture of how it all started. That it was then, and remains now from the historical point of view, the most important event or chain of events in the story of jazz in Britain can no longer be seriously denied; and a brief survey of its origins, its developments and its implications is therefore essential to our purpose.

One thing must be stressed: the revival was *not* initiated by any one band or organised by any one clique. Nor was it started by any one book, magazine, radio network or professional researcher. Its origins lie in the work of men like Derrick Turner in Britain and Wingy Manone and "Muggsy" Spanier in America—men who loved the music of the old-timers and who set about creating a demand for the same type of thing played live; in the rarity of genuine jazz performances during the "boom" days of swing, which had the effect of driving the enthusiast back to the solace of his old records; in the wave of romantic curiosity which prompted men to try and find out what had happened to the forgotten stars of yesterday. These were the roots; the bands and books commonly cited as being responsible for the revival were in fact its fruits.

In 1939 Messrs. Harcourt, Brace and Company, the New York publishing house, issued the first edition of *Jazzmen*, edited by Frederick Ramsay, Jnr., and Charles Edward Smith. The book was to revolutionise the world of jazz; in the utmost detail it chronicled the story of the music and the men who had made it, starting with the earliest New Orleans bands. "Every living jazz musician who could contribute factual material" was interviewed. "The sum-total of information obtained in this manner was then typed and made available to all the contributors. Information from different sources was carefully collated and checked. A second series of interviews followed in order to clear up doubtful points . . . then a running text which continues the narrative from section to section was written."[1]

This was a work of scholarship comparable to the most painstaking musicological researches conducted by the more serious academies. It opened up new fields; it put back into the limelight men like Willie "Bunk" Johnson, Joe Oliver, Edward "Kid" Ory and Ferdinand "Jelly Roll" Morton. And, above all, its romantically nostalgic style of writing accentuated—in those who already had it—a desire to "get back to the old stuff". And that is just what trumpeter Lu Watters did do in 1940, forming his own band on the island of Yerba Buena in San Francisco Bay.

The policy of the band was clearly laid down. The idea was to re-create the music of Oliver's Creole Jazz Band and the Morton Red Hot Peppers, flying in the face of the current belief that New Orleans music was little more than an interesting museum piece. They were to disregard all white Chicago-style music and all big-

[1] From the Introduction by the editors.

band swing; Oliver-Morton jazz was the only jazz, to which it was intended to add the Yerba Buena Jazz Band's own contribution. Such was the acclamation with which this manifesto was received, and the new band's success in carrying it out, that other groups joined the experiment and the New Orleans revival became a Movement.

It was checked when the United States entered the Second World War and the Watters band broke up. Then in 1946 they reassembled at their old home, San Francisco's Dawn Club, where they continued to attract a large number of converts until the band finally split, with trumpeter Bob Scobey and trombonist Turk Murphy forming their own New Orleans styled groups. But by his time Crescent City music had well and truly risen from the dead.

In England, Lu Watters had his counterpart in a young pianist, George Webb. It would no doubt be fanciful to assume any connection between the closing down of Storyville and Webb's birth in the same year, but the coincidence is nevertheless a happy one since he was to become, within twenty-five years, the spearhead of the European jazz Renaissance.

Webb received no academic musical education; like the great majority of British jazzmen, his enthusiasm for jazz was fired by the American records available during the '30s, and before long he was feeling the necessity of creating as well as listening. Working in a factory near his home at Bexleyheath, Kent, were amateur clarinettist Wally Fawkes and trombonist Eddie Harvey, and in 1942 the three enthusiasts were practising together, with the aid of Webb's old recordings of Oliver and the Louis Armstrong Hot Five and Seven. The following year they formed a full band, roping in Owen Bryce and Reg Rigden on cornets, Buddy Vallis on banjo, Art Streatfield on tuba and Roy Wykes at the drummer's chair. Then, conscious that their experiment was creating an interest locally, they hired a hall at the "Red Barn", Barnehurst, christened themselves George Webb's Dixielanders and offered their wares for public consumption.

Night after night the "Red Barn" was filled to capacity with eager listeners, many from London and even further afield. They listened reverently, elbows on knees and chins in the palms of their hands, for all the world as if the music was a Bach Mass and the "Red Barn" the Royal Albert Hall. And there were no dancing; Humphrey Lyttelton makes this quite clear in his autobiography *I Play as I Please*:

"Jazz was a serious music to be studied and you could not give it full attention when you were being buffeted and trampled under foot by dancers. At the 'Red Barn' people who jogged about in their chairs too vigorously were discouraged by petulant frowns from their neighbours."

By 1945 the band had more than a local following, which was suddenly multiplied ten-fold when the B.B.C. Radio Rhythm Club engaged them for a broadcast. Thousands of jazz enthusiasts all over the country were astounded to hear what seemed to them a reincarnation of the legendary King Oliver's Creole Jazz Band. The Jazz Appreciation Society and the Challenge Jazz Club organised a private record label, "Jazz", and the Dixielanders were the first to enter the studios for them. Decca then offered them a session, and their future was assured.

But there was still a great deal of opposition to the whole concept of revivalism from the influential critical clique. As early as 1941, when the nearest thing to New Orleans music was the Dixieland style of the Squadronaires, Sidney Martin was insisting that "New Orleans style went to the grave when the Dixieland Band died. Now it cannot be considered a style. . . . The history of what the early jazz was in the Crescent City explains a lot. For one thing, most of the antediluvian swing outfits were street-corner groups of slum minstrels. Drums, piano and all the other cumbersome rhythm instruments were too heavy to carry, especially when the cops weren't sympathetic."[1] This just about sums up the attitude of Webb's own detractors.

[1] *Gramophone Record,* July 1941.

In 1946 Reg Rigden dropped out and George Webb, desirous of retaining the double-trumpet lead as befitted an ardent Oliver disciple, signed up twenty-six-year-old ex-Eton trumpeter Humphrey Lyttelton to join Owen Bryce. Lyttelton was at that time almost completely unknown to the general public, and his first few weeks were marred by an understandable nervousness. First of all he did not find it at all easy to fit in with colleague Bryce, who had, over the years, fashioned his style to complement that of Rigden and was now finding it only half a style. Individualist Lyttelton was not inclined to supply the missing half and did not fit easily into the front line until Bryce left the band a few months later. This time Webb agreed to leave the line-up as it was, without implementing the group; but Lyttelton, although he played some superb jazz and laid the foundations of what was subsequently to prove a brilliant career, was never completely at his ease with the Dixielanders. His own tastes were more catholic than Webb's, and he felt an aversion to the solemn, purist enthusiasts who made up the bulk of his audience. Later that year he also resigned from the band and free-lanced for two months before forming his own group. Wally Fawkes, who had by this time developed into an excellent clarinettist with an individual style, left Webb to join him, and the Dixielanders finally broke up.

Theirs had been an enormous achievement. Armed with little more than an almost-forgotten model, a handful of variously talented musicians and all the enthusiasm in the world, George Webb had succeeded in injecting into jazz that spark of significant vitality that had been missing in British music for a quarter of a century. He was the Calvin and Lyttelton the Luther of the New Orleans Reformation in Europe.

And, indeed, it would seem that the Reformation supplies an all too apt analogy, for alongside the enlightenment schism developed. With the Barnehurst purist as prototype, there developed a fanatical sect of jazz worshippers for whom Webb and his associates existed only to be studied, analysed and eulogised in low whispers and in pretentious stereotyped quarterlies which appeared and disappeared with bewildering rapidity. It seemed that the purpose of New Orleans music was merely to provide an esoteric pleasure for a select Bohemian coterie and to spawn a new language of obscure terminological slang. At this stage these jazz aristocrats would no more have thought of dancing to their music than they would to a hymn tune. And they were flanked on both sides by the conservative old guard who were content to give custom to the co-existing kingdom of swing.

The rigidity of the newer sect was shattered when, in 1947, Graeme Bell's Australian Jazz Band paid a visit to London. Just as Watters in America and Webb in Britain had sought to re-create the music of the Crescent City, opening up new vistas and giving tangible expression to a new movement, so the Bell band had found in Melbourne another ready following for jazz in the traditional pattern. Their great opportunity had come when they were invited to represent their country at the 1947 Prague Youth Festival. To the Australians, having thus travelled half-way across the world, London seemed no more than a step away, and they made arrangements for a visit with jazz critic Albert J. McCarthy.

Nevertheless, on their arrival at Southampton they were greeted with the news that no engagements had been booked for them, and they were obliged to do a short series of one-night stands whilst fixing up with an accredited agent. A concert in the Birmingham Town Hall did much to bring them a little greatly needed publicity, but it was not until the formation of the Leicester Square Jazz Club that they really began to hit the headlines. Although by no means any less "traditional" in approach than the Webb band, they were soon revolting against the unhealthily solemn atmosphere in which their admirers were constantly forcing them to play, and eventually they hired an N.S.P.C.C. ball-room situated over Leicester Square's Café de l'Europe, where they played their jazz for dancers rather than musicologists. "Of course, no one knew anything about the dances which were originally danced to the music in New Orleans at the beginning of the century. So the dancers at the Leicester Square Jazz Club just invented steps of their own. Led by the art school contingent —the least inhibited of those present—they flung themselves on to the floor and did just the first thing that came into their heads. . . . What the diners in the Café de l'Europe below thought about it has never been ascertained."[1]

It was not long before the N.S.P.C.C. decided that its activities did not include the prevention of cruelty to jazz enthusiasts, and the Bell band was evicted. Nevertheless, they had made their point: jazz, even *real* jazz, was a functional music which lost nothing of vitality or integrity when played for dancers. Humphrey Lyttelton, whose own band had adopted the new policy, joined forces with the visitors, and both bands established their home base at the London Jazz Club in Great Windmill Street. When, in July 1948, Melbourne reclaimed her conquering heroes, Graeme Bell's Australian Jazz Band left in their wake a third faction among the warring jazz public— a middle-of-the-road faction whose creed was "New Orleans *and* dancing".

The Lyttelton band, consisting of Harry Brown on trombone, Wally Fawkes on clarinet, Pat Hawes (and, occasionally, George Webb) at the piano, Neville Skrimshire on guitar, Lew Rawlings on bass, and John Robinson (with occasional visits from Dave Carey) on drums, were the undisputed successors to the Webb and Bell crowns. But they were by no means alone in their championing of the New Orleans style. A whole host of "trad." bands appeared, as it were, from nowhere, and if London was the centre of the new upsurge of activity, the provincial cities were not far behind. The 1948 boom in amateur jazz-making was as akin to the guitar-twanging craze of ten years later in that a great deal of noise was made with very little music of

[1] Humphrey Lyttelton's *I Play as I Please*.

quality to show for it. But a handful of players did contrive to produce good music and good jazz amid the welter of fortissimo pseudo-Oliver. John Haim's short-lived Jelly Roll Kings, the early Cy Laurie Four, the Merseysippi Jazz Band and the Saints Jazz Band were all, in some measure, pioneers.

The next step forward in the search for the authentic New Orleans sound began with the formation of the amateur Crane River Brass Band at Cranford. Here, in 1949, trumpeter Ken Colyer teamed up with his vocalist brother Bill, Sonny Morris on 2nd cornet, John Davies on trombone, Ben Marshall on banjo and guitar, Julian Davies on sousaphone and Ron Bowden on drums. On the recommendation of Cy Laurie, a young clarinettist named Monty Sunshine completed the group and the title was changed to the Crane River Jazz Band.

The avowed policy of this group was to re-create the archaic jazz of the Storyville period. But they entertained no illusions as to the nature of their self-imposed task, for each was careful to make it known that "no European or anyone outside New Orleans will ever re-create New Orleans music".

The Crane River Jazz Band was nevertheless responsible for some of the earthiest jazz of early British revivalism. By 1952 Ken Colyer had become something of a perfectionist in his search for Crescent City purity and he decided to visit the jazz Mecca itself in order to meet and play with some of the old-timers who were still playing old-time jazz in the accredited old-time fashion.

Back in Southall, Middlesex, a young trombonist named Chris Barber was attracting attention with his New Orleans Jazz Band, consisting of Dickie Hawdon and Ben Cohen on cornets, Alec Revell on clarinet, Mickey Ashman on bass, Brian Baker at the piano, Ferdi Favager on banjo and Brian Lawes on drums. This group was promising to become one of the most interesting of the many out-of-town combinations when Chris Barber decided to team up with ex-Crane

River clarinettist Monty Sunshine in forming a band ready for Ken Colyer to lead on his return from New Orleans in 1953.

The new Ken Colyer's Jazzmen proved to be the finest traditional band produced by the British revival. With Lonnie Donegan on banjo, Jim Bray on bass and another Crane River apprentice, Ron Bowden, on drums, it seemed that the traditionalist camp had found a first-rate spear-head; and it was hailed as a tragedy when, a few months later, it was announced that the band was to break up as a result of a difference of opinion between Colyer and Barber.

The split proved, however, to be a blessing in disguise. Barber continued to front the old Colyer group, with Pat Halcox of the Albemarle Jazz Band in the ex-leader's place, and Ken, with his "New Orleans or nothing" determination, recruited Eddie O'Donnell (trombone), Acker Bilk (clarinet), "Dis" Disley (banjo), Dick Smith (bass) and Stan Greig (drums) as his new Jazzmen. The Colyer brand of jazz has changed little, and is unlikely to change much in the future. The new Barber band was to develop into the finest traditional-style combination on this side of the Atlantic.

At this stage, as is recorded elsewhere, it began to be obvious that British bands were no longer taking the classic Oliver records as their masters, but were tending to become shadows of either the archaic Colyer band or the smoother Barber group. Just as the Lyttleton band's one-trumpet rule had led to the redundancy of many a 2nd trumpet, so now the Colyer-Barber five-piece plan led to the eclipse of many an aspiring jazz pianist.

By 1956 it was becoming painfully obvious that the traditional field was beginning to lose direction. Too many bands were content to plug away with standard arrangements and standard improvisational clichés. One of the most noteworthy exceptions was the band led by clarinettist Sandy Brown, which, throughout 1957, pioneered the British "traditional-mainstream" type of jazz, representing a free and easy handling of the traditional conventions without breaking beyond their boundaries. Early in 1958 Sandy Brown was forced by extra-musical considerations to relinquish his leadership of the band. Whether, under the new leadership of Al Fairweather, the band will prove to be the saviour of our somewhat stagnant traditionalism, must remain to be seen.

Chapter 7

FIRE FROM THE ASHES OF SWING

A number of American musicians became dissatisfied with commercial swing, but were not prepared to switch to the traditional style. Dizzy Gillespie and Charlie Parker developed the be-bop cult, George Shearing introduced post-swing ideas to Britain, and Johnny Dankworth and the Club Eleven set the foundations for modern jazz in Britain. The West Coast "cool" style obtained a large following by means of recordings, but Modern Jazz as a whole suffered serious set-backs during the "rock 'n' roll" period.

"MODERN JAZZ" means different things to different people. In its widest sense, of course, all jazz being produced today is modern; thus "Kid" Ory and Chris Barber are, respectively, as worthy a pair of modern jazzmen as Milt Jackson and Victor Feldman. Again, the term is used in a vague sense to cover any and every field of jazz other than that produced by the New Orleans revival; but more often than not "Modern Jazz" is a descriptive title given to the new music which originated as "bop", "re-bop" or "be-bop".

We have seen how mounting dissatisfaction with the sweet swing of the '30s led eventually to a nostalgic searching into the roots of a more glorious past, which culminated in the music of Lu Watters, Graeme Bell and George Webb. But by no means all the disgruntled swing-men felt inclined to pass through the pearly gates newly opened by these pioneers. A generation spent in civilising jazz and expurgating from it its crudest Negro features was not to be flung away overnight. Thus it was that, as the revival-cum-revelation spread the gospel of King Oliver and the Crescent City, the overwhelming majority of musicians were cautious at the prospect of burning their boats behind them, and the growth of the traditionalist movement was achieved by the crusading energy of a few enthusiasts rather than any mass exodus from Swingdom to New Orleans by the players themselves. Of the musicians who did find their individuality hampered by the stereotyped demands of the pre-war public, there were few who were able to offer more than vague, non-constructive criticism, and most of them had their little moan without showing any fiery determination to improve their output at the expense of their pocket. A few of them developed into interesting individualists owing no cut-and-dried loyalty to any one particular school, attracting a nucleus of interested listeners without making any deep impression on the public or on jazz history. It was not until these anchorless seekers and unhappy wanderers recognised their spokesmen that the ashes of swing could be fanned into a second world-scorching blaze.

Five such spokesmen appeared, all of them members of the set that gathered informally at Harlem's little Minton's Playhouse club. Thelonius Monk's whole approach to the piano was fresh and original in an unforced sort of way, and Kenny Clarke's drumming was no carbon copy of any known style; Charlie Christian, electric guitarist with the orchestra led by "King of Swing" Benny Goodman, was pioneering with his own peculiar harmonic approach; and ceaselessly experimenting with him were John Birks ("Dizzy") Gillespie on trumpet and Charlie Parker on alto saxophone. Until his death in 1942, when he was only twenty-four years old, Christian was accepted as unofficial leader of the experimental faction, and it was upon Gillespie and Parker in particular that his mantle fell.

No two jazzmen constantly spoken of in one breath have ever been more dissimilar extra-musically. "Dizzy" was bright, bluff, energetic, open, happy to be alive; "the Bird" was dark, enigmatic, fiercely and fanatically musical, visionary, puzzled, and for ever struggling desperately to locate and release the music that was in him. It was Gillespie, so the legend goes, who was responsible for the christening of the new music. While rehearsing a number he burst into an exuberant shout of "Be-bop, Be-bop, that's what I want!" He got it, and Be-bop became the official name of a new jazz style. Men like Miles Davis, Lennie Tristano, Bud Powell and Jay Jay Johnson added their own contributions, and modern jazz became Modern Jazz, a safe, established route of escape from the dying world of swing. A host of critical literature appeared from nowhere, as it would seem, expressing a full range of opinion from the sarcastically derisive, through the cautious and uncommitted to the ecstatically enraptured. "Mezz" Mezzrow has put on record the opinion that he shared with many a traditional player: "If that's music I'll eat it. It reminds me of how the old-time white musicians, learning to play hot, thought all you had to do to sound hot was play very fast and with a lot of notes. And there's nothing new in these harmonic ideas. It's a waste of breath to talk about stuff like this."[1]

Be-bop gathered its first supporters from among the ranks of those who had long thought of jazz as a changing, progressive art—a chain of links in which the last was the most important. The value of jazz thus varied in accordance with its age, a point of view which was diametrically opposed to the purist-traditionalist dictum "The older the better!" and is best put over in the words of British modernist Ronnie Scott: "Traditional jazz was the result of Southern United States environment of Negro immigrants. 'Chicago' style was the result of this new Negro art-form on white Americans. A direct line may be traced, via Armstrong, Teagarden, Goodman right down to so-called modernism, which is only the latest link in a chain of musical evolution. . . . Modernism, with its technical virtuosity and comparatively academic approach to harmony in jazz, is the result of

[1] *Metronome*, October 1946.

better instruments, cheaper musical education, and a revolt against the exceedingly narrow limitations of traditional jazz harmonies."

George Shearing was probably the first British jazzman to introduce the post-swing ideas to this country, as he had previously been the first to introduce the newly rediscovered "boogie-woogie" piano style back in 1938. Born blind on August 13th, 1919, he had studied music at the Linden Lodge School for the Blind, free-lanced round the smaller London clubs from 1935 onwards, and had made his first records under the Decca label only two years later. But before he was able to develop into Britain's first distinctive protagonist of the modern style he emigrated to America in 1947. At this time British enthusiasts—and musicians, which accounts for the loss of Shearing—were finding it increasingly difficult to keep abreast of new developments; American bands were still to be heard on records only, the 1935 feud between our Musicians' Union and the American Federation of Musicians being still very much alive; and to make matters worse only a small proportion of American issues were allowed into Britain before 1949, by which time many of our progressively inclined musicians were reduced to picking up their ideas at second-hand from the more fortunate jazz fraternity on the Continent. In the meantime, a large number of potential adherents had fallen under the dangerously exclusive spell of Stan Kenton and his big-band music of the future. Nevertheless, there was a slowly growing demand here for the new music, as evidenced by the reception accorded to the Gillespie recordings issued by Parlophone in 1947. Edgar Jackson, writing in the *Gramophone* (June), was not too wide of the mark when he prefaced a dissertation on the eccentric new trumpeter with the assertion that "Gillespie has created among British swing enthusiasts more interest than any other contemporary American swing celebrity".

It was this growing interest and demand which ultimately brought together eleven bop-inclined musicians for the purpose of establishing a British equivalent of the Minton research and development centre. Led by alto-saxists Johnny Dankworth and Ronnie Scott, the Club Eleven groupings were to bring into prominence such men as trumpeter Reg Arnold, pianist Dennis Rose and guitarist Pete Chilver, by means of concerts in the Birmingham Town Hall and London's Kingsway Hall, and also through the records issued by the enterprising Esquire label on which they featured. Dankworth and Scott were fired by their close aquaintance with the American trends, obtained by working for a period on the transatlantic passenger liners, and they were able to lay a solid foundation for modern jazz in Britain.

But in spite of the fact that the new ideas were finding a ready public, there was as yet no financial incentive to the British musician, and such modern groups as were formed came together, for the most part, for isolated concert, club or recording dates. The big bands of Ambrose, Ted Heath and company were providing a livelihood for most of the men who were to dominate the modern scene within a few years; a handful of small groups featuring nothing of interest to the jazz enthusiast were cashing in on the "progressive" craze and labelling themselves "be-bop bands", confusing and eventually antagonising the public; and it was not until 1950, when Johnny Dankworth formed his Seven, that modern-styled jazz became a force to be reckoned with in this country.

With Dankworth himself on alto and Don Rendell on tenor, Jimmy Deuchar on trumpet, Eddie Harvey (the same as had made his name with George Webb's Dixielanders) on trombone, Bill le Sage at the piano, Eric Dawson on bass and Tony Kinsey on drums, the Seven was, in its early days, one of the few units on this side of the Atlantic which contrived to pursue an original course which was experimental without being cerebral. Leader Johnny proved himself a composer of exceptional talent and an arranger of many and varied capabilities, a perennial source of inspiration to his less-gifted colleagues. But the public was lamentably slow in giving credit where credit was due; the more superficially exciting music of the Vic Lewis Orchestra, with its Kentonesque "new sounds", was attracting one wing and the new Long Playing records, presenting the American Modern Jazz giants in an attractive format, was luring away another. The Johnny Dankworth Seven were forced to come into line to a certain extent, but it is to their credit that in doing so they contrived to retain their place of pre-eminence in the British scene. Their more "commercial" numbers were interlarded with jazz that *was* jazz, and a steady following was slowly and painfully built up—a following which proved to be of considerable value to the groups which took over the market when the Seven was temporarily disbanded and Johnny entered the big-band world.

His Club Eleven colleague Ronnie Scott also played no little part in establishing an audience for live modern jazz, first with his small groups and later with his own large combination. The Ronnie Ball (later Tony Kinsey) Trio developed a restrained, unpretentious style which stood them in good stead whether playing under their own name or supplying rhythmic backing to larger units. Young "child prodigy" Victor Feldman fulfilled all his early promise as a drummer, and in addition developed his talents on piano and vibes— the latter to a quite extraordinary degree. Modern jazz was beginning to stand squarely on its own feet when the Rock 'n' Roll craze was introduced here by Bill Haley and his Comets with vocalist Elvis Presley. This phenomenon is discussed in a little more detail elsewhere; here it will suffice to mention that more than one musician of note turned to the craze as a golden opportunity for making a little money, and the modern jazz scene suffered a slump. Now that, at the time of writing, Rock 'n' Roll appears to be in decline, most of the prodigals are returning to the jazz fold. Whether or not our modernists will succeed in establishing a stable base upon which they can build still remains to be seen after nearly ten years of conjecture.

In the early '50s it became evident that there was developing on America's west coast a new brand of modern jazz in which form was all-important, emotional expression was rigidly eschewed and arrangements were tight, cerebral and ruthlessly epigrammatic. At the centre of the revolution were baritone saxist Gerry Mulligan and drummer Shelley Manne, both of them creating a large following in Britain by means of their records. It cannot be denied that the majority of modern fans give their support to the "cool school", but the style has never been thoroughly explored by British musicians. Most of our modern enthusiasts are in the somewhat paradoxical position of having a better knowledge of the Dave Brubeck Quartet or the Modern Jazz Quartet than they have of Tony Kinsey or Victor Feldman.

Most British modern men have similarly avoided the one hundred per cent experimental or "far out" varieties of jazz, and its enthusiastic followers have again been restricted to the recordings made by American units. It would seem that the Modern Jazz scene in Britain is suffering from too many musicians without a public, and too many enthusiasts without any opportunity for hearing "live" the music they are prepared to buy on record.

Chapter 8

LOOSE ENDS

The cleavage of opinion dividing the jazz world into two co-existing camps is an artificial one. Historically, the existence of a number of widely differing schools and phases must be recognised, even if it is argued that one school is of more aesthetic value than another. The jazz field continues to widen.

THE civil war in which the jazz world became engulfed with the almost simultaneous rise of the new modern and traditional camps reached its climax in the middle '50s. It was not, of course, purely a British phenomenon—the same sort of split had occurred in America and on the Continent—but here the struggle was conducted at an altogether higher pressure. They were few and far between who protested an equal validity for both schools of thought, running the risk of being labelled appeasers, sitters on the fence. And the pages of the jazz magazines were filled with facile "proofs" that one or the other was the only style worth worrying about.

It is a far cry from the Original American Ragtime Octette to the Tony Kinsey Quintet. George Lewis would have considerable difficulty in recognising in Jimmy Deuchar a colleague working within the confines of the same art, and it is tempting to wonder just what sort of reception the chanting plantation slaves of a hundred years ago would have accorded Lonnie Donegan's Skiffle Group. But unless we are able to see all these as members one of another, fruits of the one tree, we run the risk of contracting a sort of critical myopia which will distort all sense of perspective and pervert our one permissible object, that of enlightened enjoyment.

This is a plea for the validity, and indeed the necessity, of an historical approach. Thus we can be quite convinced that jazz is a New Orleans folk-music which began to disintegrate during the First World War along with the conditions which brought it into being, without in any way denying the historical importance of later developments. Or again, we can insist that all but a few dozen American musicians are constitutionally incapable of creating real jazz, without denying that an elementary knowledge of the British product will, at the very least, help create that sense of perspective and proportion which gives anchorage and solid foundation to our judgment. After all, no man writes an English history leaving out all the battles just because he happens to be a pacifist, or ignoring all the kings and queens because he happens to be a republican. And, whether we like it or not, there is such a thing as the British jazz scene.

But to insist that all sorts and conditions of schools and styles, wings and factions, must be apprehended by the eye of the historian is not to pretend that we ought to be capable of extracting from all of them an equal quantity of enjoyment (if enjoyment can be considered quantitatively). Some are mutually exclusive; if we admire A for aiming at X, we are going to be irritated by B, who is devoting all his energies to the suppression of X. But our understanding and consequent enjoyment of the art of A will be enlightened by a knowledge of the work of B; and if we continue in our belief that B is barking up the wrong tree, then at least our criticisms will not be the result of a blind prejudice and might even begin to have constructive value.

In the foregoing brief history, then, we have traced the development of jazz as it has occurred in the British Isles. That practically all such development has been the result of American influences—through gramophone records and visiting musicians—not even the most fanatical patriot could deny. Nor is this to be regarded as conclusive evidence that there is no such things as good British jazz. As we have had occasion to mention, the music of the "Spike" Hughes recording groups, deeply influenced as it was first by Red Nicholls and then by

Duke Ellington, can hold up its head with the best. The question of whether or not Britain has succeeded in maturing her own distinctive style will be discussed at a later stage in this book.

In four decades of one form or another of jazz the music has left an impact on every strata of British society: on the aristocratic "Mayfair set", where since the early '20s it has been a necessary accompaniment to sophisticated cocktail parties; on the working man and his girl, who form the backbone of today's jazz clubs; and even on the stupid, dull, conventional, dry-as-dust *Bourgeoisie*, who seem to have supplied most of our top-of-the-bill jazz musicians. No art or entertainment, with the possible exception of Italian opera, has been so consistently abused, ridiculed, preached against and scoffingly consigned to a premature grave; nor has any sphere of music been so persistently and wilfully misunderstood; none has engendered such blatant snobbishness; none has produced so many newspaper headlines. In the mind of many a respectable man jazz is equated with drink and drugs and all the rest—"I've got nothing against the music, but it's what goes with it." And in spite of all this its popularity continues to grow and its impact becomes all the more solid and sure.

Jazz has reflected or expressed an outlook that seems to be peculiar to the twentieth century—as other musics have done for their own time. It has had an almost incalculable effect on our popular entertainment music—modern dance music, film music, variety music and the "pop" song. Today it is as much at home in the Royal Festival Hall as it is in the dingiest Soho cellar; in the University common-room as much as in the factory's social-hall. It scrapes its way from the distorting throats of the old portable gramophones and leaps into tiny drawing-rooms from enormous hi-fi combinations. Its characteristic melodic phrasings reappear in Ravel's piano concertos and in the errand-boy's whistle. At a time when virtually nothing is certain, this is certain: that jazz history will continue to be made for many years yet. And some of it will be made in Britain.

A summary of historical events which have had a bearing on
jazz in Britain

1848 Visit of Major Dumbledon's Ethiopian Serenaders, introducing imitations of American Negro music.

1873 Visit of Jubilee Singers of Fisk University, introducing genuine Negro spirituals.

1907–12 Occasional infiltration of ragtime.

1912 Visit of Original American Ragtime Octette, sparking off the craze for syncopated dance music.

1914–17 The characteristic music of New Orleans begins to spread northwards.

1916 It is christened "jazz" in Chicago.

1917 The term is introduced to London and the first British group to describe itself as a "Jazz Band" is engaged at Murray's Club.

1918–21 The novelty aspect of jazz catches the British imagination and supersedes ragtime.

1919 Visit of the Original Dixieland Jazz Band, introducing jazz on the New Orleans model.

1921–22 Public dissatisfaction with "novelty jazz".

1923 Visit of Paul Whiteman's Orchestra, introducing "symphonic syncopation".

1926 *Melody Maker* first published.

1927 Significant increase in number of American records released. Introduction of the term "Hot Jazz" to differentiate between the music produced by small semi-improvising groups and the fully arranged music on legitimate lines. Publication of first book on jazz to appear in Britain: R. W. S. Mendl's *The Appeal of Jazz.*

1928　Fred Elizalde opens at the Savoy Hotel and introduces various American "hot" men to Britain.

1928–30　Gradual enlightenment of the British public due to the continued availability of American records—particularly of Red Nicholls and the New York school.

1930　Elizalde returns to Spain. "Spike" Hughes makes his first records. The Ted Lewis Orchestra visits Britain.

1932　Visits made by Louis Armstrong and "Fats" Waller.

1933　Visit of Duke Ellington. Second visit of Louis Armstrong. "Spike" Hughes makes his last records.

1934　Visit of Joe Venuti. Publication of Constant Lambert's *Music Ho!*

1935　Small groups almost completely superseded by big bands. The term "Hot Jazz" gives way to "Swing". Dispute between Britain's Musicians' Union and America's Federation of Musicians, resulting in a ban on visiting American bands which was to last twenty years.

1936　Visit of Benny Carter as arranger to B.B.C. Dance Orchestra.

1937–47　British jazz scene dominated by pseudo-Dixieland groups such as the Squadronaires.

1938–40　New Orleans revival had its beginnings in America.

1943　George Webb's Dixielanders assemble at Bexleyheath.

1945　The Dixielanders attain a nation-wide following.

1947　Graeme Bell's Australian Jazz Band visit Britain and re-introduce jazz for dancing.

1948   Humphrey Lyttelton forms his own band. The bop movement begins to get under way in Britain.

1949   The traditional school is firmly established.

1950   The modern school finds a spearhead with the formation of Johnny Dankworth's Seven.

1951–57   Continual growth of traditional school. Continual fluctuation in the fortunes of the modern school.

1953   Ken Colyer introduces a revival of the early New Orleans style.

1955   The dispute between the two unions is finally settled.

1956   Visits made by Stan Kenton and Louis Armstrong. The "Rock 'n' Roll" craze weakens Modern Jazz.

1957   Visits made by Gerry Mulligan, George Lewis, Count Basie, Jack Teagarden, Eddie Condon and the Modern Jazz Quartet.

II

TABLE TALK

Red Nicholls, whose early "Five Pennies" recordings pioneered the field of "hot jazz" in Britain during the late 'twenties.

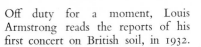

Off duty for a moment, Louis Armstrong reads the reports of his first concert on British soil, in 1932.

Duke Ellington, whose 1933 visit had a profound effect on British "big band" jazz.

The early Webb band which was to revolutionise British jazz in 1945 with its "back to New Orleans" policy.

Chapter 1

WHAT IS JAZZ?

Numerous attempts have been made to evolve a definition, but none of them has been entirely satisfactory. Jazz must be viewed in perspective against the background of music as a whole—the background of folk-music, art music and the various forms of commercial music.

SINCE jazz was described in 1919 as "a piece of music entirely surrounded by noise", innumerable attempts have been made to give it some sort of definition, if only to protect it from the vague free and easy thinking which associates all popular music with jazz. There have been the technical definitions which describe the music in terms of rhythmic and harmonic structure; the sociological definitions which describe it in terms of a particular place and a particular time and particular circumstances; the epigrammatic definitions designed to impress rather than instruct. There have been the one-sided definitions which have picked out certain elements of jazz and equated them with the whole—"Jazz is rhythm" or "Jazz is playing the way you feel"; and there have been dishonest definitions, put together for the purpose of proving a predetermined point. There does not seem to be one among them all that can really do its subject justice, and it is certainly not my intention to formulate one, or to lay down a set of rules and regulations. Jazz, like lacrosse and the expanding universe, has its boundaries, but no one really knows just where they are.

On one point we must be quite clear from the outset. We are asking ourselves What is Jazz? not What ought Jazz to be? Thus we must disregard as a point of departure any such assertion as that jazz is jazz only when it conforms to a certain ideal pattern. We may argue passionately that the only worth-while music is the music of the soil, the common folk, the people who feel before they think; or we may be convinced that of all music the noblest is that in which a sensitive civilised mind consciously explores its medium and slowly, painstakingly pieces together an expressive and significant sound-pattern. But to insist that the only music to come under the jazz umbrella is that which corresponds, more or less, with our own ideals is like insisting that brunettes are something less than women because one happens to prefer blondes.

It has been suggested more than once that jazz is a method of playing music rather than a music in its own right. There is a strong element of truth in this; "Bobby Shaftoe" is not a jazz tune, but it becomes one when played by Chris Barber's Jazz Band. Even "When the Saints Go Marching In"—in regularity of performance the Beethoven's Fifth of jazz—started life as a hymn tune. But there have been hundreds of directives given by composers in order that their music might be played in a particular way. None of them has achieved the status of a distinctive school in the same way as jazz has done. And even if we capitulate completely and accept it as a truth that jazz is an ordinary music played in an extraordinary way we have still to examine the nature of that way, which brings us back to where we started.

A far more popular school of thought which seems to have come to the forefront in the early days of the New Orleans revival, and which we have already had cause to mention more than once, seeks to explain jazz as a folk-music, or more specifically as *the* folk-music of the American Negro. This is, of course, by no means far-fetched; jazz has its basis in the blues, the spirituals and work songs of the Negro folk, and still owes much of its character to these. But the symphony and the oratorio, the opera and the string quartet also have their origins, if we go back far enough, in the music of the people.

And whatever else they may be they are certainly something other than folk-music.

"Folk-lore", the term which was to give birth to "folk-song", "folk-dance" and "folk-music", has been in use for little more than a century. Musicologists in England, when they talk of folk-music, refer to the traditional musical heritage of a specific race or culture. Folk-tunes cannot be attributed to any one composer, since they have matured over the years, sometimes over the centuries, constantly changing and dividing into new sequences and continually embellished by scores of hands. Unfortunately, the American musicologist has stripped the term of its significance by using it in a vague and all too comprehensive sense to cover virtually all but concert music and music composed as aesthetic exercise. In this latter sense, jazz is certainly a folk-music; as Louis Armstrong comments, "I ain't never heard no horse singin'!" In the stricter English sense, it is not.

Nevertheless, it partakes of the nature of folk-music to a far, far greater degree than does "classical" music. A great deal of the raw material of jazz is traditional, in much the same way as is the folk-tune; the blue notes are a perversion of the pentatonic scale on which most Western folk-music is founded; a finished piece of jazz is the result of a collection of personalities or a collective personality rather than the creation of one man interpreted by others; and improvisation, the basic constituent of folk-music, plays a vital part in the creation of jazz. But to suggest that the work of the Johnny Dankworth Seven is folk-music is to extend the meaning of the term to a point at which it has even less significance than the American distortion. And to excommunicate the Seven from the company of the elect is to fall into the error that we have just denounced: that of unduly limiting our definition.

It is particularly fashionable today to regard jazz as an art-form—a plastic medium by means of which an artist can express himself. We are assured that just as the symphony developed from folk-music via instrumental interludes, suites and overtures into the lofty form which has provided means for the communications of a Beethoven, a Mahler or a Sibelius, so jazz has developed from the blues via brass bands and what-not until today it is competent to express emotions and reactions which have hitherto been expressed within the framework of the other fine arts, if they have been expressed at all. So far so good; but there is still a very real difference between so-called art music and jazz. Art has as its object communication—communication not of emotions or reactions, views of life or ways of looking at things, but something other and beyond these which has no literary equivalent. Music is of all arts the most abstract. It communicates only itself. The substance and the means of communication are one. Beethoven's "Eroica" does not merely communicate heroic emotion, it communicates the "Eroica". And when emotions are aroused in one listener, they will differ in degree and kind from the emotions aroused in someone else by the same piece; they will certainly differ from Beethoven's own emotions as he wrote the work.

Not all "classical" music comes into this category; a great deal is produced with the simple object of entertaining, and that is something to be thankful for! But art music does exist primarily as a vehicle for the type of abstract communication which we have been thinking about, and jazz just does not come into this category. It has always been first and foremost a functional music accompanying parades and dances. No one can sensibly deny the immense value of jazz as a means of expression, nor that there are many jazz performances on record which are miniature jewels of musical art. Some of us will not be afraid to claim that the creative genius of "Jelly Roll" Morton was equal to that of Chopin.[1] But we nevertheless insist that the

[1] Both were essentially creators of impromptu and pseudo-impromptu dance-music. Both used the piano as their primary medium. Both suffered neglect during their lifetime. Both were acclaimed as geniuses after their death.

essential purpose and function of jazz is altogether different from that of the "classical" music world.

Again, it has been claimed that jazz is nothing more than a rather eccentric brand of popular entertainment music. It is produced, the cynic will tell us, because it lines pockets, fattens purses and puts bank balances somewhere in the region of the stratosphere. Any value that it has is to be measured in terms of £ s. d. rather than by any aesthetic standard. This point of view has grown as a result of the popular identification of the word "jazz" with any and every mani-festation of "pop" music—a misconception which is discussed more fully in another chapter. It has never been advanced by the reasonably knowledgeable critic; the sketchiest survey of jazz history makes it abundantly clear that, for the most part, jazz musicians have been struggling to make a living out of their music, stubbornly insisting on playing as they felt rather than obsequiously bowing to mass taste. And yet, again, we are compelled to admit that there are points of contact between jazz and the other stuff with which it has been identified. Jazz has made no little use of the commercial "pop" song; there has been more give and take between jazz and commercial music than most jazz fans care to admit; and twice within its first twenty years as a mature music it came within an ace of degenerating into a wishy-washy artificial hybrid music, first with the symphonic syncopation craze and later with swing. But the contact between genuine jazz and Tin Pan Alley has been in the nature of a harmless flirtation rather than a more serious courtship.

To gather in the threads, then, jazz is something of a folk-music but not a folk-music, something of an art music but not an art music, something of a commercial music but not a commercial music. It is, in fact, unique. There is nothing else quite like it, or if there is it has yet to develop into anything more than a local curiosity. Its uniqueness lies primarily in the peculiar tension between the folk element of improvisation and the sophisticated art element of prearrangement. These are the twin rocks upon which the whole superstructure of jazz is erected, and every piece of jazz combines the two to a greater or less extent. Sometimes the improvisation element will dominate, as in the celebrated jam session where pre-arrangment plays only a small part (but is nevertheless present even when contributing nothing more than a basic snatch of melody); and sometimes a piece will be so fully arranged as to be to all intents and purposes a fully fledged legitimate composition, retaining improvisation only as an influence—as an aural illusion. It is surely worth a mention that the two Negro bands which have received most critical acclaim, King Oliver's Creole Jazz Band and Morton's Red Hot Peppers, combine the two elements in so extraordinarily subtle a degree that it is virtually impossible to say where one leaves off and the other starts, the tension between them resulting in a total effect which is quite different from that produced by either folk or art music.

Improvisation is something more than "playing as you go along". It is a method of composition and is, in fact, at the source of all composition. Arranged music is the baby of the arts, boasting a life span of a few hundred years compared with the thousands in which the literary, pictorial and plastic arts have developed. The artist who expresses himself in literature can construct on paper a pattern of words which results in his finished work of art; in painting, a pattern of colour and form is projected on to a canvas. But in music the artist has no concrete medium in which to construct; he must create his pattern in sound waves and arrange that pattern, not on paper or on canvas, but in time.

Small wonder that music lagged far behind her sister arts when there was no way of recording it other than by means of the human memory. But things changed a great deal when a method of musical notation was worked out. The improvising-and-remembering performer was now able to record his work on paper by translating it into a visual language which could be retranslated in terms of music by other performers who had never actually heard the piece. And, more important, the artist could work out in advance the pattern of sound he intended to convey. He could construct complicated part-songs and instrumental pieces. So, by translating the illusive language into a concrete language which could be set down on paper, the musician was able to explore more thoroughly than ever before the science of his art, constructing in visible signs a more and more complex architecture of sound and then translating it back into the language of sound. Thus the whole basis of prearrangement, of conscious composition, or interpretation lies in the advent of musical notation.

The difference, then, between improvisation and prearrangement lies in the fact that the one is musical thinking translated directly into patterns of sound and the other is musical thinking which is first translated into a language which can be committed to paper, where it is then shaped and polished at leisure, emerging only at a later stage as living music. It is the tension between these two principles which makes jazz the unique music that it is.

Improvisation never died out, even when the revolution effected by notation had swept all before it. It remained the vital constituent of folk-music simply because a large section of the community never learned to read a score, and it was only when industrialisation tore at the throat of tradition, and science and universal literacy combined to standardise thinking and outlook, that folk-music began to disappear, and improvisation with it. But it has also survived to a small extent in art music. Until well into the nineteenth century it was by no means uncommon for orchestras to be kept together by a harpsichordist who filled in the harmony and generally punctuated the written score at will. During the eighteenth century the prima donnas of Italian opera were granted a great deal of freedom in elaborating and embellishing their arias, and composers of instrumental concertos made plenty of allowance for the improvised cadenza of the soloist. Since the late-nineteenth-century elevation of art into

Art, all this has disappeared and the modern concert pianist is more inclined to use a prearranged cadenza rather than improvise a real one on the spot. Mozart's concertos are very often played exactly as written, in spite of the fact that the composer intended the soloist's score to be no more than a basic outline for embellishment and creative performance. Improvisation would seem to be virtually a dead art, made use of in the modern concert-hall only by way of freakish novelty, as in Carl Neilsen's Fifth Symphony, where the side-drummer is instructed to let loose "as if at all costs he wants to stop the progress of the orchestra". Only in the conservative sphere of organ music is real improvisation incorporated into the scheme of things, and even here it tends, in the hands of all but two or three masters, to be nothing more than a reshuffling of the tunes in "Hymns Ancient and Modern".

In the face of this it seems quite incredible that the great majority of musicologists will have nothing whatsoever to do with jazz, the only living music to preserve all the glories of improvisation. One would think that they would at least take an academic interest in it. And all the more so since New Orleans jazz incorporates not merely sequences of improvised solos, but collective improvisation in which the musicians follow their own melodic lines, creating one indivisible network which is a great deal more than the sum of its parts. That a music of intense beauty and urgency can result from what are, by modern textbook standards, utterly naïve and haphazard methods, is due to the oneness achieved by basing the improvisation on a simple harmonic scheme and a simple ground rhythm. In addition, each participating musician develops an intuitive understanding of both his medium and his colleagues without which the end product is likely to be collective chaos. Although in post-New Orleans jazz the concept of collective interplay has tended to give way before the simpler basis of successive solos, improvisation has remained the constant keynote.

Jazz is what it is as a result of the conditions in which it was cradled.

As we saw in the very first chapter, it is the effect of many causes. Traditional Negro music came into contact with a sophisticated civilised music, as every folk-music in Europe has done. It had always been the folk-music which had wilted and buckled under the strain of co-existence, surviving only as a new influence in the music which had conquered it. But by a million to one chance the Negro music reversed the process; it was powerful enough to absorb and transform the hitherto unconquerable giant. It had never happened before, and the resultant new music was unique; but it did not fit into any category devised by the academic mind, so it was ignored.

Ignored by the musicologist, but not by the people. Throughout the white world jazz has found a niche and satisfied a need. When folk-music became no longer a living force and the world shrank with the advent of new means of communication, a new all-embracing, cosmopolitan music became a necessity. Art is not, never has been, for all. But they are few and far between who can dispense with all music, and for those who saw nothing in the sterile and artificial stuff which was churned out of the Tin Pan Alley sausage-machine, jazz was the answer. Its function was that of the old folk-music: to accompany song and dance. It was (in a literal, not the religious sense) a non-conformist music for a non-conformist age; a melancholy music with a glittering façade; a music of protest and revolt; a crazy music for crazy people living in crazy times.

"And this, and so much more."

Chapter 2

THE ENGLISHNESS OF ENGLISH JAZZ

Although it began as a specifically national music, jazz has developed internationally. Just as a Chicago style developed as a result of Chicago musicians imitating the New Orleans pioneers, so a British style developed as British musicians drew inspiration from the records made by those pioneers. The Chris Barber band was possibly the first English group with a distinctive English atmosphere, and the number of its imitators justify our talking in terms of an individual British style.

FIVE hundred years ago the world was flat. If you sailed out far enough you just toppled over the edge. A journey to the centre of the earth meant a trip to Rome; India was as far as heaven and hell.

Today we can breakfast in New York and dine in London on the same day. A man in Melbourne with his ear to a radio set can hear the chimes of Big Ben a split second before the people crossing Westminster Bridge. We expect to send an ambassador to the moon very soon. As we had cause to remark at the end of the preceding chapter, ours is a shrinking world.

Had it always been as it is today it would be reasonable to expect all nations to be living as members of one family, speaking one language, thinking the same thoughts at the same time in the same way. But supersonic aircraft and radio are still novelties. For thousands of years communities have lived in relative isolation from each other, developing along independent lines. Conditions determined by climate and location have in turn conditioned outlook and temperament; and because climate and geographical features vary, outlook and temperaments vary, and communities become foreign to each other.

It is only natural that the national characteristics of a people should be apparent in its art. For one thing, different characteristics lend themselves to different forms so that the genius of the Italian is most perfectly expressed by the voice, of the English by poetry. But more than that, there is something in the body of English *music* which makes it different from the body of Italian music, something in the mass of Italian *poetry* which makes it different from English poetry. It is the difference between the Mediterranean and the Atlantic, between a peninsula and an island. And because national characteristics are most clearly defined among a country's peasant folk, where there is least contact with foreign influences; and because of all folk-arts music is the most popular—folk-poetry having very little independent existence, and work in a visual medium being largely confined to the primitive image-worshipping peoples—it is in a nation's folk-music that its essential spirit is most clearly reflected.

Composers of art music have never ceased to draw inspiration from the traditional music of their native land, and this tendency has become very much more marked in the present century when composers, desperately searching for an anchor in tradition which will nevertheless leave them freedom to express themselves in the contemporary situation, have found their goal in the dying music of a dying class on their own doorstep. Thus the Borodin-Mussorgsky school in Russia, the Bartók-Kodály school in Hungary and the Holst-Vaughan Williams school in Britain have reopened and systematically explored routes which were only tentatively trodden by Vivaldi and Haydn. Other composers—Brahms with his "Hungarian Dances" is the most obvious—have made use of certain characteristics of folk-music for exotic effect, or even, as did Mozart with his "Musical Joke", for comic relief. Jazz also, because it has grown out of the folk-music of a particular race in America, has been used in a similar way. Composers as different as Gershwin and Ives have taken it as a foundation upon which they have hoped to build a national music, and a large number of European composers have been attracted by its novelty.

But because jazz is, in origin, an American music, the question arises as to whether or not its idiom can be fully absorbed by other countries with an altogether different musical background. It has been made quite clear that jazz was the product of a specific environment, and a very American environment at that. Can it survive when uprooted from that environment and transplanted, say, to England? Can there be, in fact, such a thing as English jazz?

This is very far from being the first time that the question has been raised, and more than once it has been answered forcefully in the negative. To expect jazz to flourish away from its birthplace, we are told, is as logical as to expect plums to grow on pear trees. Unless we duplicate in England the conditions which brought jazz into being in the Deep South, we shall never achieve anything more than a sterile, lifeless imitation of jazz. And since it is absurd to attempt to re-create such conditions, English jazz must remain something of a paradox.

Up to a point, this argument is irrefutable. We can be certain that neither England nor Europe—nor America for that matter—will be able to re-create *as a living music* the brand of jazz nurtured in Story-ville. But jazz is a developing organism; since it first moved north-wards from the Crescent City over forty years ago it has encountered a host of new inhibiting conditions vastly different from those which were responsible for bringing it to birth, and it has overcome every one of them. That it has undergone change in the process is only to be expected. When its home base shifted from New Orleans to Chicago, it became the property of a new set of musicians with new attitudes and a new background. The result: a new style of jazz, a metamorphosis of New Orleans style and the Chicago environment. The same sort of thing happened in New York. And, although most of us are slow to realise it, it has happened outside America.

When George Webb's Dixielanders revived the style of music featured by King Oliver's Creole Jazz Band the imitators were distinguishable from the imitated only in so far as the quality of their music was concerned. As the revival gathered momentum and an understanding of the various forms within the traditional jazz idiom developed, a host of British bands were formed and disbanded in bewildering succession. Humphrey Lyttelton pursued an individualistic path which was too free and easy for the strict New Orleans enthusiast, and his mantle as Britain's No. 1 jazzman was taken over by trombonist Chris Barber, who assumed leadership of the Ken Colyer band in June 1954, when Colyer left to pursue his George Lewis style with enthusiasts of a like mind. Barber's sympathies were wide and his musicianship was virtually unequalled. Although sticking broadly to the New Orleans tradition, his admiration for the mood and sound of the early Ellington orchestra found its way into his own music, sometimes intentionally, as in the haunting "Saratoga Swing",[1] but very often in places where one would expect a straightforward Oliver treatment, as in his rendering of the old master's "Chimes Blues".[2]

But an Ellington tinge was by no means the only characteristic which set the Barber band apart from its contemporaries. Monty Sunshine proved to be no less of a thinking musician on clarinet than was his leader on trombone, and the ringing beat of banjoist Lonnie Donegan was remarkably clear and clean. But it was—and is today—the distinctive style of arrangement associated with the band which clears them of the charge of musical plagiarism. In this, Barber has learned from Morton and Ellington and has not been afraid to apply his lessons in an original and individual way, so that his band has a sound which is quite unmistakable *and quite different from that of the Negro groups which have provided most of the inspiration* for British traditionalists.

[1] Recorded on Tempo EXA 22. [2] Recorded on Decca LF 1198.

It can hardly be claimed, of course, that one band alone can justify our speaking in terms of a national style. But it has now become obvious that the characteristics which we have associated with Chris Barber's Jazz Band have been appropriated by scores of traditional bands all over Britain. The bands of Terry Lightfoot, Alex Welsh, Bobby Mickleburgh and Eric Silk have learned as much from Barber as from Oliver, and a whole host of amateur groups are striving after the Barber sound. Just as in the early '20s Chicago style developed when the white Chicagoans imitated the great bands that were coming north from New Orleans, so British style has developed during the '50s as a result of British musicians imitating the records of those self-same bands. In the latter as in the former case, the imitation developed until it could exist in its own right. Thus we can say that, historically, Chris Barber is the Bix Beiderbecke of British-style jazz.

Whether or not this British style will eventually be considered of any permanent value is for a later generation to decide. Our point is that, whether we like it or not, whether we believe in it or not, whether we support it or not and whether we consider it good or bad, it exists. And it exists because jazz, having found itself in a new environment, played by and for people with a new background, must of necessity be changed. The Englishness which permeates the music of Purcell, Boyd, Sullivan, Elgar, Delius and Vaughan Williams will find its way into jazz, do what we can to prevent it. And Britons never shall be squares.

Chapter 3

"TRAD." AND "MOD."

Traditional Jazz, a music of the 'twenties, has been written off as an anachronism as played in the 'thirties. Its non-conformist character, however, justifies its continuance as a contemporary form in this non-conformist age. A large proportion of the Modern Jazz output is produced with the idea that complexity and aesthetic value are linked.

It might be as well, at this stage, to turn our attention towards some of the controversies which have centred around the revival of New Orleans jazz in Britain.

The hundred and one arguments which have hotly denounced or deified the music can be, for the most part, assigned to one of four categories. First there are those which deprecate the whole conception of revival as an anachronistic putting back of the clock, and these sometimes find allies in the second category comprising those which dismiss the revival on the grounds that it has produced no music of comparable quality to that which it attempts to revive. Alternatively, there are those which assert that the music of New Orleans is the only worth-while jazz and that it is now our responsibility to preserve its traditions in as pure a form as possible. And the final category joins in pressing for the validity of the revival, but insists on the necessity of developing along new lines if traditional jazz is ever to be more than an empty relic of bygone days.

Taking these in order, the attitude of deprecation stemming from a conviction that New Orleans jazz in the '50s is a fish out of water is expressed succinctly by Maurice Burman writing in *Jazz Journal*.[1]

[1] May 1950.

"As much as I love good New Orleans music," he argues, "it does not belong to this age, and it does not sound the same as it did in the '20s. If you want to know why it doesn't, you must study Einstein's theory of relativity. The music on the record is the same, but everything around has changed and therefore in relation to the new conditions the music itself changes." It follows that a British enthusiast listening to a hi-fi performance of a Red Hot Peppers number is going through a very different experience from that of the Chicago Negro who, thirty years earlier, bought the first copy off the press. His musical and aesthetic background, his pattern of experience, indeed his whole world, is entirely different. But a realisation of this all too simple truth does not give us the prima facie right to assume that the experience of the one is any more or less valuable than that of the other.

There could hardly be a more complete antithesis between the attitude and outlook of an eighteenth-century open-air audience tapping their feet to a Mozart divertimento and that of a present-day audience listening to the same piece, chin in hand, in the Royal Festival Hall. The music will "mean" something utterly different to each of them, but the "meanings" cannot be compared or assessed in terms of value. The music of, say, Michael Haydn, Ludwig Spohr and Cipriani Potter, which was of real significance to their contemporaries, is now for all practical purposes dead because, as the outlook and conditions which originally made it acceptable underwent change, it became apparent that the appeal of the music was rigidly bound within the framework of those conditions, and was thus unable to change with them. There we have a basic difference between music that is "great" and music that is merely good; the appeal of the one is such that it remains constant in spite of change in external conditions, whereas the other, though it may be highly significant to the public for whom it is originally composed, will lose its foundations when that public changes. New Orleans jazz has taken root in England in a way that none of its pioneers would ever have dreamed possible. We

Dancing to New Orleans jazz was more or less unheard of before Graeme Bell brought his Australian Jazz Band to Britain in 1947. Here, Harry Varney (g) and his wife Marie, Don Roberts (cl), Russ Murphy (ds), Adrian Monsbourgh (tb), and Roger Bell (co) arrive in London.

Harry Brown, Humphrey Lyttelton and Wally Fawkes preaching the doctrine of revivalism in 1948

can only assume—whether we ourselves "see anything in it" or not—
that the music has a significance for the modern British enthusiast
which, if very different from that apparent to the American Negro
thirty years ago, is none the less valid for all that. In other words,
whilst finding nothing to argue about in Mr. Burman's last two
sentences, we must insist that the conclusion stated in his first is by no
means a logical consequence.

Our second category of controversy embraces those arguments
which deny the usefulness not of the revival itself but rather of
revivalist bands. It is conceded that the growth of interest in the
infancy of jazz and the resultant research which produced such books
as *Jazzmen* have been of real value in building up a balanced understanding of the music and its history, and, further, that the rehabilitation
of Keppard and Oliver, Dutrey and Dodds and a host of others has
long been overdue, whilst the return in the flesh of old masters such a
"Kid" Ory and "Bunk" Johnson has put a seal on what would otherwise have existed only on paper and on wax. But this, continues the
argument, is as far as the revival ought to go; it ought to be a revival
of interest in the old-time music rather than a revival of practical
music-making in the old-time style. Because New Orleans jazz
is no longer the spontaneous, living music it once was, modern bands
playing in the traditional style cannot hope to improve upon the
existing corpus. The contemporary musician should therefore adopt a
contemporary style. But to insist—and this argument implies such an
insistence—that the demand for music in the Crescent City pattern
ought to be fully satisfied by the old recordings is to deny the basic
function of jazz. Jazz is dance music, and you cannot expect people to
dance to the strains of a gramophone, particularly when the turntable
is occupied by an ancient, patched-up Gennett—or even a Long
Playing reissue. If the revival of interest in New Orleans jazz is going
to be anything more than an uprising of historical awareness, a quirk of
the academic clique, then people are going to want to dance to it. And

if people want to dance to New Orleans jazz, bands must exist to play New Orleans jazz. Provided that they play it with a reasonable degree of competence—and, generally speaking, the public seem to be supporting those that do and ignoring those that do not—and fulfil their function of providing dance music in a worth-while style, who are we to complain?

It might be—it has been—protested that these revivalist bands are not content with satisfying jivers in the clubs, but must also invade foreign territory by putting their essentially imitative product on record, thus presumptuously inviting direct comparison with the old masters. Whilst it is by no means an entirely satisfactory state of affairs that a British group outsells Louis Armstrong, this does no more than prove what has long been apparent in any and every comparable sphere; namely, that there are always the people who perversely insist on preferring paste to diamond. When a local band finds itself with a personal following, it is only natural that it should seek to enhance its own reputation, spread its fame and improve its finances by this means. If its music has "got something", nothing is lost; if it has not, it will not last long anyway.

On the opposite side of the House are those arguments which offer vociferous approval for any and every manifestation of the New Orleans spirit. It is here that we encounter the arch-purist, the man who believes that there is no jazz but the jazz of Storyville and all else can go hang; Chicago style is New Orleans in its first stage of decadence; swing carries the decadence a good many stages further; and bop is beyond the pale. The Johnny Dodds Washboard Band exemplifies New Orleans style at its furthest permissible stage of development; Oliver's Creole band and the Red Hot Peppers show it at its smoothest; George Lewis presents it at its purest. The revival is delightedly hailed as a return to sanity after a couple of decades of irresponsibility. But—and this is where the purist is distinguished from the common or garden "trad." man—it is dogmatically asserted that mere traditionalism is not enough. It must be the right sort of traditionalism. Any departure from the strict New Orleans line is out of the question. In other words, the New Orleans style is frozen—put in a state of suspended animation; any development of it is unacceptable because once it *is* developed it no longer belongs to New Orleans.

Unfortunately, we cannot have our cake and eat it. If there is no jazz but the jazz of New Orleans as it was early in the twentieth century, then there can be no revival, for that New Orleans has gone for ever. To insist on reviving a music and then freezing it in a particular phase of its development is to court certain failure. You just cannot play around with history like a cat with a ball of string. If New Orleans style must be revived, it must be revived as a living, developing, growing music; otherwise all freshness will be lost and any improvisation will become a sterile rehashing of clichés.

This is, in fact, the argument which we have placed in the last of our four categories. It has been championed by the majority of critics, who have long been complaining at the lack of originality and distinctive personality in some of our British bands; and not least by such musicians as clarinettist Sandy Brown and trumpeter Humphrey Lyttelton, who, whilst showing a proper respect for tradition, have refused to become the slaves of it. Where their individualism will lead them is anyone's guess. "As a practising musician," writes Lyttelton in his autobiography *I Play as I Please*, "I am often asked 'Where do you propose to go from here? You can't just stand still.' The only answer that any musician can give to this is the Irishism, 'If I knew where I was going I'd be there now!' "

The "We don't know where we're going until we're there" dilemma is by no means the prerogative of the traditionalist. It is even more acutely apparent in the modern camp, which is preoccupied not only in a search for goals but also for routes by which the goals might be approached. Indeed, it would seem that neither the "trad."

nor "mod." man is content to live in the present. The one must dig into the past, the other must peer into the future; the inspiration of one is the music of a long-lost Golden Age of Jazz, and of the other a "music of the future" in which half a dozen decades of jazz are eventually consummated. The symbol of the traditionalist is a spade, of the modernist a crystal ball.

The principle which motivates the world of modern jazz is a belief in progress. Jazz is an art-form; an art-form must progress; jazz must progress; Q.E.D. Like so many assertions made by jazz critics, this is a plausible half-truth. As we have already seen, it is impossible to freeze a music in any particular phase of its development and then expect it to continue to flower freely. Since music, along with every-thing else, has for centuries changed with changing years, successive phases budding and blossoming, decaying and dying, we do not have to be numbered among the three wise men to prophesy that jazz will fall in with the established pattern. But it is an error of the first magnitude to equate technical development with aesthetic improve-ment, which is just what has been done time and time again, and is still being done by practising musicians, professional critics and enthusiastic listeners. It is announced that, because Bill Bloggs and his Bloggheads have done something new—something which no one has ever thought worth doing before—they must henceforth be regarded as a "significant" group. The result of such an attitude is that novelty is pursued for novelty's sake and each group searches for, and claims to find, a "new sound", a "new direction", with "new possibilities". Thus the central ambition of the musician who is bitten by the futurist bug is to discover and to pioneer the next historical phase, rather than the simpler but far more praiseworthy aim of producing down-to-earth decent music.

This is not to decry experimentation. There is some truth in the idea that technical (as distinct from aesthetic) development is largely a matter of trial and error. But the whole thing is reduced to an absurdity when experimentation becomes an end pursued for its own sweet sake. The legitimate experimenter is the musician who finds himself so cramped by the currently prevailing style and language that he is forced to seek new means of expressing himself. And this is just how significant change has occurred throughout musical history; certainly not as an end product of a "Let's find something that no one else has ever done before" attitude.

"New means of expressing himself." The sort of progress with which the modern jazzman is legitimately concerned is purely and simply technical development—new instrumental combinations, new tone colours, new harmonic or rhythmic foundations, new architectural forms. If and when he succeeds in his search, it does not mean that the music he produces is intrinsically more valuable, or "better", than the average piece of music fashioned within the framework of the older convention. If it has any meaning at all, it is that this particular musician is now able to produce better music than he himself would have been capable of producing if he had remained tied by the prevailing rules and regulations. His music is probably also better than that of other musicians who have elected to stick to the older convention, overriding a conviction or an intuition of its sterility because it is financially profitable to do so, or because it is expected of them, or through mistaken notions of loyalty. But there may be dozens of musicians who are *perfectly satisfied with the current language and perfectly able to express themselves by means of it*, and these may well produce better if more old-fashioned music than our experimenting friend. All of which means that the music of Tony Kinsey, in spite of being a good deal more "modern", is not necessarily better than that of Chris Barber.

Another popular fallacy is that which rates value according to a sort of scale of complexity. I have quite frequently sounded friends by putting to them the old question, "Why do you consider a Bach concerto to be 'greater' music than a Tin Pan Alley popular song?"

Time and time again the answer has boiled down to the observation that the Bach is more complicated than the "pop" piece. Similarly, there are a large number of enthusiastic modern jazz fans who rate Charlie Parker and Johnny Dankworth above "Bunk" Johnson and George Webb on the grounds that their music happens to be the more complex. Even if this supposition is established as fact—and a good case could be made for reversing the verdict—it proves nothing in so far as the intrinsic value of the music is concerned. Webern's music was considerably more complicated than Haydn's, but the latter has lasted for a couple of centuries without showing any sign of dying, whilst Webern's stuff has proved to be, for the most part, still-born. Music, including jazz, is a language. That is, it is a means of communication. Complexity is therefore a vice rather than a virtue. It is justified only when the matter to be communicated becomes incommunicable without it. Bach's concertos and Bartók's quartets are "great" in spite of, rather than because of, their complexity. The same is true of a great deal of modern jazz. Any attempt to use technical complication as a yard-stick for judging aesthetic value is to be fiercely resisted and written off, for the most part, as intellectual snobbery.

That there are modern jazzmen who are free of the diseases of novelty-seeking and technique-worship no one will seriously doubt. To point out that a large proportion of modern jazz is rubbish, produced by charlatans who have deceived themselves into believing that they really are restlessly-seeking geniuses is not to decry the field of modern jazz as a whole, still less to damn it with faint praise. There are the men who really do think along original lines without consciously striving for something new to say. We shall come back to them and to their traditional colleagues in the last chapter of this section, when the whole future of jazz will be reviewed.

Chapter 4

THE FIELD OF PSEUDO-JAZZ

Commercial music is nothing new. Since the early rag-time days, it has borrowed a number of the character-istics of jazz and is still indistinguishable, in the minds of the general public, from jazz proper. Modern popular song is a mass-produced commodity, an erotic pill coated with the sugar of music.

IN days of old when folk-music was in its heyday and art music was virtually confined within church walls, there were a number of men in Britain, and more particularly on the Continent, who made a living by travelling from village to village entertaining the locals with a repertoire of ballads and songs—and passing the hat round at every opportune moment. Because it *was* their living, they naturally aimed at satisfying the tastes of their clients rather than improving their appreciation of music; the cheap piece that elicited a good response and filled his hat was of more practical value to the wandering minstrel than the most haunting melody which had no appeal for the unmusical, and consequently the musician whose primary aim was to make money found that this was most easily done by concentrating on the lowest musical intelligence in his audience. Bad music which filled a hat was a better proposition than good music which only half-filled it.

The minstrel, then, put music into the category of commercial commodities, made it into an article of trade. Its new status became much more marked when growing industrialisation drove a large proportion of peasants and countrymen to the towns and cities. Here the commercial music was cut off, as the music of the minstrels was not, from the purifying and vitalising influence of the main mass of folk-music, and it developed in its own sour way, motivated by nothing but the law of supply and demand; supply being in the hands of musicians whose primary concern was their pockets, and demand being that of a public who delighted less in beautiful music than in lecherous lyrics, and who preferred to have their tunes studded with easily recognisable clichés rather than exercise their minds on anything outside established convention. In short, a third camp joined the long-established entrenchments of folk and art music: music for the unmusical.

The new trend would seem to have reached maturity in Regency London, when the sale of popular music was backed by a network of rival business enterprises—not so very different from the pattern to which we are accustomed today. When Queen Victoria came to the throne and inspired a long era of surface respectability, the drawing-room ballad, eminently suitable for well-bred young ladies to play on Papa's piano, became the most important commercial music of the day. Towards the end of the century the gravitational centre of popular music, under the influence of the lighter Viennese school, shifted to the dance-hall or ball-room, and also to the music-hall. So was created a climate conducive to the acceptance of the syncopated music known originally as "ragtime" which made numerous attempts to establish itself in Britain during the first decade after Victoria's death, succeeding, as we saw earlier in this book, just before the First World War. In the ball-room, as in the restaurants and hotels, it put a new pep into dance music, and in the music-hall it provided a new inspiration for comic songs. It was not until after the war, however, when ragtime and syncopation became "jazz", that this commercial music for the unmusical grew to the gargantuan proportions to which we have since become accustomed.

Before the arrival of jazz and since the eclipse of folk-music, commercial music was essentially a child of the concert-hall and the opera-house, though the inheritance was watered down to such an extent that the parentage was barely recognisable. When jazz came in with such a flourish, it was pounced upon by those whose sole interest in music was bound up with the prospect of financial gain, and the love-child of the illicit union of diluted jazz and filthy lucre was the modern "pop" song. When Sir Henry Coward produced his famous denunciation of jazz in 1927 it was this pseudo-jazz that he had in mind; they were few and far between who could distinguish the imitation from the real thing, or who realised that both existed. And it was not until the end of the decade that the musical profession coined the term "commercial music".

Why this unprecedented boom in unmusical music? There were various reasons. For centuries the population had consisted of educated and uneducated in sharp contradistinction. The educated listened to music either because they enjoyed it or because it was the done thing to show some measure of appreciation; the uneducated had their folk-music. Then, when folk-music was pushed out as industrialisation set in, a vacuum was left. Not until jazz provided the perfect spring-board from which operations could be launched was the vacuum adequately filled—not by jazz itself but by the pseudo-jazz which grew out of it. Again, such mechanical contraptions as the gramophone and radio have broken down the old rule of utility—"If you want music you must make music"—by providing it at the touch of a knob, and this has had the effect of standardising a whole nation's supply and demand.

Since commercial music severed its tenuous ties with the concert-hall and opera-house and became the parasite of ragtime-cum-syncopation-cum-jazz, most of it has either come directly from America or has closely imitated the American styles. The vague, mushy sentimentality of the Victorian drawing-room ballad was superseded by the extroverted boisterousness of the equally superficial pseudo-jazz. The prudish attitude of the Victorians with regard to sex matters was now in retreat, and it was not long before the lyric-writers were joining hands with the rest of the entertainment world in cashing in upon the gradual relaxation of unhealthy inhibitions. Practically every song dealt with love—of sorts. "In modern songs", wrote Constant Lambert in a much-quoted paragraph from *Music Ho!* "it is taken for granted that one is poor, unsuccessful, and either sex-starved or unable to hold the affections of such partner as one may have had the luck to pick up. Even when the singer says that he has a woman crazy about him he hastens to point out that her attitude is clearly eccentric and in no way to be expected." Pornography has not infrequently found its way into lyrics—and I refer to songs on the ordinary market, not the obscene stuff which remains under the counter—and a technique of double meaning has been developed to perfection so that sexual emotion can be aroused or portrayed without the risk of incurring condemnation by the law. This aspect of the music is apparent not only in the printed words of a song but also in its presentation. To be a smash hit as a "pop" singer it is more important to exude sex-appeal than it is to be able to sing in tune; vital statistics provide a surer qualification than academic training. The technique of the intimate approach—the husky whisper, the passionately embraced microphone, the implied invitation—these are the hall-marks of modern commercial music, the music which the public insist on regarding as jazz.

On top of this is the preoccupation with matters technical. Ragtime songs not infrequently contained passages in praise of ragtime, and this procedure has been adopted consistently ever since. Thus we are advised that "Everybody Does the Creep", "I Never Felt More Like Singing the Blues", "I Got Rhythm and Blues", "We're Gonna Rock . . ." and so on. This is a form of publicity—where a song contains the publisher's blurb within the framework of its own lyric —which would certainly seem to be confined to the unmusical music of the twentieth century or pseudo-jazz. To quote Lambert again:

"Folk-songs do not inform us that it's great to be singing in six-eight time, or that you won't get your dairy-maid until you have mastered the Dorian mode. . . . What should we think of a concert aria which kept harping on the fact that the singer's mouth was open and that her vocal cords were in prime condition?"

We have noted that "big business" is behind the pseudo-jazz market. The truth is that not only does the business world control the "pop" *output* but it also controls public *taste*. A particular type or style of song is put on the market with such a barrage of publicity that the public is almost hypnotised into response. The Tin Pan Alley tycoons are shrewd enough to realise that their most profitable line of attack is the exploitation of fashion consciousness. Thus, when one song proves to have some appeal, the market is flooded with a whole host of similar pieces. We have seen fashions for semi-religious songs, for French-styled songs, for songs of the American Civil War, for "Rhythm and Blues" numbers, for "Rock 'n' Roll" and calypso-rhythms. As each fashion reaches its height of popularity, the businessmen prepare another to take its place, and the tragedy is that the public are, for the most part, quite unaware of the appalling quality of the goods they are buying and genuinely convinced that their music has the merit of tunefulness and is therefore more worth listening to than all "that rowdy classical stuff".

Most popular songs originate in or off London's Charing Cross Road; importations start their British careers there. Practically all of them are written by men under contract who assemble songs in their offices in much the same way as others assemble motor cars on a factory belt. There is no effectual contact whatsoever between manufacturer and consumer. The songs eventually chosen for recording or publishing as sheet music are foisted on the public by gigantic plug campaigns, and those which achieve national popularity are sorted into an ever-changing "top ten" or "top twenty" league table. Few and far between are the numbers which contrive to retain their place within this hierarchy for more than two or three months.

Two schools of commercial music deserve more than a bare mention. Skiffle is an offshoot of traditional jazz, and because, in its modern form, it is a distinctively British product and because also it is a great deal more than a run-of-the-mill music for the unmusical, it has been granted a full chapter to itself. The notorious "Rock 'n' Roll" style also started life as a jazz offshoot featured by such American groups as the Big Dave Orchestra and Bill Haley's Comets. In 1954 the latter group featured extensively in the film "Rock Around the Clock", and the new style of music with its heavy, purposeful rhythm, frantic riffing and hypnotic electric-guitar solos swept America. Most of the numbers which subsequently hit the headlines were available in Britain during 1955, but it was not until the film had its British release the following year that any real impact was made. During its opening run, teenagers established the precedent of jiving in the cinema gangways. When this was clamped down upon, they jived in the roadways outside the cinema after each evening performance, literally rocking "around the clock . . . 'til the broad daylight". Then the press got hold of it and front pages were filled with colourful stories and pictures with the old, old accent on "decadent youth". Provincial cinema managers who wanted a quiet life refused to show the film, and those who jibbed at foregoing the luxury of a packed house took the precaution of calling in the local police "just in case". The inevitable result was that the general public went to the cinema not to see the film but rather to witness newsworthy disturbances; and the "Teddy boys" went to satisfy them.

Because of all this, the music has a bad reputation to live down. Nevertheless, if the truth be told, the earlier numbers were infinitely more wholesome than the sloppy, slobbery, semi-sacred ditties or the huskily whispered sex-songs which until then occupied the centre of the stage. The form was, of course, a very limited one, and within a few months anything of value in it had been exhausted; nevertheless, when it can be seen in perspective I believe that, with all its faults, it will be judged one of the least obnoxious of the fifty-seven Tin Pan Alley varieties.

Just where commercial music will go from here is anyone's guess. Certainly it will continue to flourish in one form or another while there is a market for the third-rate and a demand for sex dressed up in music. George Orwell pictured the "pop" song as being turned out, in the year 1984, by "an instrument known as a versificator", the songs being "composed without any human intervention whatsoever". Perhaps he is right; and perhaps the songs of 1984 will be all the better for it.

Suffice it to say that if we want to see genuine jazz music accorded the recognition it deserves it must be disassociated in the public mind from the music of Hollywood or Denmark Street. In recent years some advance in this direction has been made, but nothing like enough. Jazz is a living music, produced for the love of it; commercial music is an artificial commodity, produced for the money in it. In essence, they are as far as East from West. And, in essence, never the twain shall meet.

Chapter 5

SKIFFLE

Skiffle is the modern "music of friends". It has its roots in the "spasm music" of late eighteenth century New Orleans and has developed via the blue-blowing groups and jug bands of the 'twenties. Modern skiffle is often little more than American folk-song with rhythm accompaniment, as popularised by Ken Colyer and Lonnie Donegan. It has suffered as a result of identification with "rock 'n' roll". Its future may well lie in a return to the traditional blue-blowing techniques.

SKIFFLE is do-it-yourself music; it is the chamber music of jazz, and there is no better description of it than the following passage by Edwin Evans written apropos "classical" chamber music in A. L. Bacharach's *Musical Companion*: "The most admirable recent definition of the term . . . is that which describes it as the music of friends. Though much of it is now performed in public, it is essentially the music of those who come together to make music for themselves, as distinct from those who gather at concerts to have music made for them." The distinction may not be apparent to the many thousands who confine their skiffle activities to the buying of records or the journey to Greek Street, but it is there nevertheless.

Furthermore, skiffle in its modern form is essentially a British product—British in that it is more or less confined to the British Isles. When Bill Haley was busy introducing rock 'n' roll to Britain, Lonnie Donegan was attempting to sell skiffle to the Americans. That it has many of the hall-marks of popular American music none would deny; but there is such a thing as naturalisation. This is not to perpetuate the ridiculous heresy, propagated by the women's magazines and their

126

kith and kin, that skiffle started with Lonnie Donegan. The popular young Irishman is no more the "Father of Skiffle" than was Haydn of the symphony or Buddy Bolden of New Orleans jazz. Skiffle has its history, and that history, if it is very sketchy and static compared with the over-telescoped evolution of full-blooded jazz, is none the less as deeply rooted. Again, like that of jazz, it has no cut-and-dried beginnings; we cannot pinpoint a year in which it was invented, nor can we trace its source to any particular person or place. We talk of *the* source of a river, but every river has sources without number.

The "spasm bands" of New Orleans were the first recognisable precursors of modern skiffle. They were, for the most part, street bands which entertained passers-by in the French Quarter of the city at about the turn of the century, providing their music by means of such utility instruments as old bottles, tin cans, jugs, lead piping and the occasional luxury of a legitimate banjo or zither. They took over the prevailing musical language of proletarian New Orleans—the language that was just beginning to flower into a homogeneous jazz music—and belched it out with enthusiastic gusto. None of these bands is remembered today, but the pseudonyms of some of the musicians—Warm Gravy, White Whiskey, Stale Bread—speak volumes on the nature of their music to those who have ears to hear.

Alongside the spasm bands we must place the minstrel-tradesmen. Molly Malone, wheeling her barrow through streets broad and narrow and attracting custom for her sea-food by boldly singing its praises, was well and truly outclassed by her competitors in New Orleans. The rag-and-bone man and the itinerant tinker, the waffle-pedlar and the fruiterer each attracted attention to his merchandise by extolling its virtues in impromptu ballads and blues, often accompanied by percussive beats on tin cans, water-bottles or ribbed washboards. Jos. Mares, Snr. (Jnr. played in the famous "Papa" Laine band), who has lived in New Orleans for more than eighty years, reminds us of "the old bottle man who frequented the Negro neighbourhood in the vicinity of Clairbourne Street" and who "tooted his tin horn at every stop of his pushcart, announcing his arrival to nearby residents and that he was ready to trade any old bottles for a stick of taffy-candy or some gew-gaw. The horn used by this bottle man was the ordinary type of tin horn used during the carnival parades. Only one tone was possible from the blast of this instrument, but the old bottle man contrived, through some wizardry of his own, an amazing trick enabling him to blow several tones or notes which he would blast forth in a jerky or syncopated manner." This was no chamber music, it is true; nor was it skiffle. Nor did it ever evolve into anything more elaborate, being in due course swallowed up within the main stream of jazz. But if this was a false start, it was nevertheless a start of sorts. The spasm buskers and the candy man were the grandparents of skiffle.

Their music seems to have fallen further and further into the background as the more legitimate forms of jazz obtained an increasing hold on the New Orleans population. It had its heyday when jazz was in its infancy stage and still something of a novelty. The same sort of thing seems to have happened when the best musicians transferred the centre of jazz from New Orleans to Chicago during and immediately following the First World War. Again it was the novelty aspect of the music which attracted attention; all its most superficial and bizarre characteristics were copied by the local whites, and jazz music found its way into the rent parties which were a regular feature of the poorer quarters of the city in the '20s—the era of Prohibition and Al Capone. These parties were thrown by luckless tenants on their finding themselves in arrears with the rent, and they took the form of an informal *soirée musicale*. Guests would bring along their own musical instruments, and those who were unable to play would join in by humming into comb-and-paper combinations, snorting into jugs and buckets or pounding away on the wife's washboard. Then, in the early hours of the morning, when the primitive jam

Cy Laurie re-creates the music of Johnny Dodds at his Soho club.

Chris Barber.

session came to an end, the hat came round and the rent was collected by subscription.

Such impromptu music was not particularly revolutionary; small-time amateur music of almost any sort was known throughout the Great Lakes area as "skiffle"—as it is today in many parts. What *was* new was the jazz flavouring. The comb and paper, particularly in its mechanical kazoo form, provided a popular means of cashing in on the jazz craze for those unwilling to submit themselves to the discipline of learning a legitimate instrument, and in the middle '20s commercial skiffle groups were formed. By far the most famous of these were Red McKenzie's Mound City Blue Blowers, who started life as a trio in 1924 and, as we have seen elsewhere, visited Britain, where they were instrumental in sparking off the craze for the industrial kazoo bands which took some of the hellishness out of the hell of the subsequent depression. Most of the effects which have been associated with blue blowing were used at some time or another by the Mound City group, which McKenzie managed to keep in business, in spite of continuous changes in personnel, throughout the '20s and into the '30s. The fact that such men as Eddie Lang, Jimmy McPartland (with brother Richard), Eddie Condon, Jack Teagarden, Glenn Miller, Coleman Hawkins and "Pee Wee" Russell stepped into a band which was led by a comb-and-paper enthusiast speaks volumes for the status of embryonic skiffle at its best.

During the '30s the blue-blowing vogue seems to have blown itself out to a large extent, and this is hardly surprising since improvised jazz itself had a struggle to remain on the map. The washboard continued to be used to good effect in some quarters, and Tony Sbarbaro, who had wielded the drumsticks in the Original Dixieland Jazz Band, made a notable comeback on kazoo. But throughout the '40s and during the first decade of the New Orleans revival movement in Britain, skiffle was an unknown name and an unknown music except to a handful of jug-band and blue-blowing enthusiasts.

At what point the tide can be said to have begun to turn will depend upon just how rigid a definition of skiffle we decide to adopt. As early as 1949, a group known as the London Blue Blowers, led by kazooist-vocalist Bill Bailey, was working on the revivalist front, but its music was crude and commercially unsuccessful. In September 1951 Chris Barber made "Everybody Loves My Baby" and "Whoop It Up" for Esquire records (10-180), which were issued as by Chris Barber's 'Washboard Wonders' in November of the same year. With Ben Cohen on cornet and Alec Revell on clarinet this may be dismissed as just another record in the revivalist idiom, but Brian Lawes on washboard and Ferdie Favager on banjo combine to provide an atmosphere which is more informal than that of Barber's full New Orleans Jazz Band, and Barber himself plays string bass instead of trombone. This is not skiffle à la Greek Street, but the old Chicago set would have seen in it a closer affinity to the music of Red McKenzie than to that of Joe Oliver. Two years later Chris Barber's New Orleans Jazz Band was disbanded and the young trombonist teamed up with clarinettist Monty Sunshine to form a band ready for trumpeter Ken Colyer to lead on his return from a pilgrimage to New Orleans. Colyer was keen on introducing to British audiences his repertoire of folk-songs and vocal blues, and it was decided that this was best done by a small group picked from the full band. Before the idea could materialise, Colyer and the rest of the band had parted company, as told elsewhere in this book, and skiffle was propagated on two fronts —first by the new Colyer band, and again by the older group now operating under the leadership of Chris Barber.

Ken Colyer, then, was the initiator of what we might call folk-song skiffle, and when his new band made its recording debut in November 1954 with six titles on a ten-inch L.P. (Decca LF 1196), three skiffle numbers ("Midnight Special", "Casey Jones" and "K. C. Moan") were added by the skiffle group consisting of Alex Korner on guitar and mandolin, Mickey Ashman on bass, manager Bill Colyer on washboard and Ken himself providing guitar accompaniment to his own vocals. But the latter numbers went virtually unnoticed; because this was the first of the Jazzmen's records, the full-band numbers created the most interest and stole what limelight there was.

Perhaps it was unfortunate also that Chris Barber produced his first folk-song-cum-skiffle numbers at precisely the same time as Colyer and in the same format. Barber was fortunate in having behind his front line a young banjo and guitar player with an extraordinary repertoire of Negro song, and it was natural that Lonnie Donegan should assume leadership of the skiffle department. Two numbers, "Rock Island Line" and "John Henry", were sandwiched between six full-band pieces, and once again it was these latter which attracted most attention since traditional enthusiasts were keen to find out just how the Barber men would cope without Colyer. Oliver King, reviewing the record for *The Gramophone*, made much of these six numbers: "Never can such beautiful music have been made in England by a local band as is to be found on this disc. . . . Relaxed, never tense but always exciting, never rushing or increasing the tempo, nor yet dragging it, this band must be acknowledged as Britain's greatest, indeed perhaps even the greatest anywhere today"; but the skiffle numbers received no mention whatsoever and were seemingly destined to remain as obscure items of the catalogue columns.

But not for very long. If the reviewers were not disposed to spend much time on them, the jazz enthusiasts who bought the record for its jazz content were captivated by the two railroad songs, and these were soon making occasional appearances on B.B.C. request programmes. Then Decca issued them on a standard 78 r.p.m. disc, and within a few weeks they had rocketed into the "top ten" hit parade. Donegan suddenly found himself a teenagers' idol and skiffle became a household word; hitherto fanatically enthusiastic trad. men took up the cudgels in defence of the new offshoot; scores of skiffle groups sprang up both in London and in the provinces, and mail-order firms advertised skiffle sets for sale. The skiffle revival arrived with a bang.

When Lonnie Donegan left Chris Barber for an American tour, skiffle began to move from the jazz-club world to the variety stage and the world of commercial music. Leader Donegan himself accelerated the trend on his return, much to the bitterness of those who had idolised him as an obscure jazz vocalist, and the trad. intelligentsia renounced skiffle itself as a degenerate music. But by now its hold was unbreakable. Barber found a replacement for the young Irishman in America's Johnny Duncan, who, handicapped though he was by a complete ignorance of jazz music and the blue-blowing vogues, nevertheless managed to make creditable use of his own extensive repertoire of New World folk-song. Indeed, Barber's band again became the primary skiffle workshop, since Duncan's use of Western and other non-Negro material paved the way for the use of English, Scottish and European folk-song.

Most of the new skiffle groups which sprang into being modelled themselves closely on the Lonnie Donegan pattern. The instrumental debauchery of the Chicago jug bands had given way to a simpler music on a narrower pattern—folk-song accompanied by a trio of guitars plus string bass and washboard. The woodwind and pseudo-woodwind instruments which had been part and parcel of the make-up of such groups as the Mound City Blue Blowers were eschewed by modern skifflers as relics of the traditional jazz which some proclaimed themselves to be superseding. The folk-songs themselves were taken from the recorded examples left by some of the old blues singers of the '20s, and in particular, as was very much the case with Lonnie Donegan himself, from Huddie Ledbetter or "Leadbelly", who had been discovered in a Louisiana prison by musicologist John Lomax, who not only recorded a tremendous number of the earthy artist's ballads and work songs but also persuaded the authorities to grant Ledbetter a free pardon (he was serving a life sentence for murder).

It is unfortunate that skiffle came into its own in its new form just as the rock 'n' roll craze was at its height. Two separate and distinct schools of popular music peacefully co-existing was a phenomenon without precedent, and it was not permitted to last very long. By their ill-informed publicity the popular press spread the notion that the two were in fact one and the same thing, and some groups fell into line and actually effected some sort of merger. Thus Lonnie Donegan's "Gamblin' Man", in spite of a typical skiffle opening, develops into artificially worked up rock 'n' roll at its worst, and other groups of humbler rank have followed suit by adapting actual rock 'n' roll tunes to a skiffle instrumentation. In the same way the common or garden "pop" song has exercised a good deal of influence, as is seen in Donegan's "Puttin' on the Style". There is nothing folksy about this; it is a "pop" song with skiffle accompaniment and is only saved by the fact that it is a remarkably *good* "pop" song— we all know the hypocritically respectable young lady who

> . . . goes to Church
> Just to see the boys

and

> The young man in the hot-rod car
> Driving like he's mad,
> With a pair of yellow gloves
> He's borrowed from his dad.

But British skiffle did not entirely succumb to the siren call of commercialism. Groups such as that led by Ken Colyer were, and are today, content to provide the traditional repertoire of Negro folk-music in a perfectly simple and unpretentious manner, but only a few groups are, as yet, turning back to the Chicago conception of skiffle and attempting to effect some sort of amalgamation of blue blowing with Donegan style. Of the few, however, mention must be made of Russell Quaye's City Ramblers Skiffle Group, which stands head and shoulders above any other combination in the skiffle world. Well known to London's own skiffle intelligentsia, this group is as yet just one among many to the general public, who probably find the kazoo and trumpet-mouthpiece effects a little crude after the professional slickness of a Lonnie Donegan. The man in the street, in fact, is as yet unable to take his skiffle neat; he must dilute it with three parts of water.

Can skiffle ever become a music of any real value? The question cannot be answered with a dogmatic "yes" or "no". Those who apply the term to the modern British brand and are completely unaware of the fact that skiffle has existed in one form or another for over sixty years may well reply in the negative. But we would do well to recognise the close similarity between the position of skiffle today and that of jazz forty years ago. Skiffle has suddenly achieved national popularity here after some years of a relatively obscure existence, just as jazz did in America during the First World War; the popular conception of skiffle is today as wide of the mark as was the popular conception of jazz in 1917. Skiffle has "gone commercial", but the gold remains beneath the dross, as did the gold of "hot jazz" in the days of symphonic syncopation. Maybe we shall witness a similar resurgence of the happy-go-lucky essential skiffle; maybe the jazz world will again turn to a "music of friends". How this might be possible is a matter which cannot be discussed except within the context of the future of jazz as a whole. And that demands a chapter to itself.

Chapter 6

THE FUTURE OF JAZZ

We cannot prophesy but we can set out possibilities.
With the present division in the jazz world we ought to
think in terms of one future for traditional and another
for modern jazz. In the last analysis the future lies with
the musicians and not with the armchair theoreticians.

HE is a rash man who will set himself up as a jazz prophet.
There have been many of them in the past, and time has
proved almost all of them false. As we have said a little earlier,
if jazz musicians knew where they were going they would be there
now. And it is with the musicians that we must leave the future;
jazz forms are not created within the pages of books or monthly
magazines. So this chapter is neither a prophecy nor an excuse for
idle conjecture, but quite simply an attempt to list a few possibilities.

We live in a future-conscious age. Our children are taught their
history but their eyes are on the moon, the planets, artificial satellites,
rocket-ships and space-stations. The world of their imagination is a
world of the future, symbolised by an intrepid Dan Dare and an
inescapable Big Brother. The arts are by no means free of the infection,
as witness the odd conglomeration of "futurist" phases which come
and go with the monotonous regularity of Central Line tube trains
in the rush hour. We plot the future by plotting the past and continuing, as it were, on a dotted line. We take note of trends, we
analyse them and we utter our predictions; then we wait; then we
wonder where we went wrong.

The truth is that there are all sorts of unforeseeable factors with a
bearing on the future of jazz. We may decide in fine detail just how

we would *like* jazz to develop, but our plans will not be taken into account by any jazz genius who happens to rear his head, impressing a new musical vision upon his hearers and pointing a new direction with new possibilities. Again, jazz cannot be isolated from its environment; changes in the latter will father changes in the former. If the Chancellor of the Exchequer were to impose a crippling purchase tax on trumpets, clarinets and trombones in a fit of pique against jazz and jazzmen, a new brand of jazz exploring the tonal range and timbre of the penny whistle might well take over the stage. And, perhaps most important of all, it must be remembered that jazz is just one little island in the world of music and its future is bound up with the future of music as a whole.

One of the first things we must do if we are to think at all about the future of jazz music is to decide which jazz it is we are considering. For it is no longer possible for us to talk glibly about "jazz" as if there were only one music known by that name. There is "traditional" jazz and there is "modern" jazz, and since neither of these shows the slightest inclination to die off, leaving the field to the other, we must think not of one but of two jazzes; therefore not of one but of two futures.

In so far as the New Orleans pattern of music is concerned, we may be pretty certain that in two or three decades from now it will continue to be played in very much the same manner as it is today, and indeed as it has been in one place or another for half a century. New Orleans jazz has been accepted as an end in itself since the Second World War revival, and there will always be those who are content to re-create jazz at its folkiest and its most vehemenently non-conformist. The music that was cradled in red-light Storyville is something more than a primitive springboard for the plushy sounds of a Glenn Miller orchestra or the angular cavortings of second-rate mod. men. It is a mature music in its own right and a music which is capable of kaleidoscopic variety. It is a period music and yet a modern music; its language is of yesterday, but its content is for today. But this is not to deny the inevitability of development within the New Orleans and basically traditional idiom, for not all musicians will be content to remain ruthlessly bound by predetermined rules and regulations. Some will play free with the tradition that is their inspiration, either retracing the history of jazz in their own development as, for instance, has Humphrey Lyttelton, who at the time of writing is flirting with big-band jazz after passing through successive New Orleans phases, or developing their own individual offshoot of the traditional language as has the Sandy Brown band. The latter possibility is perhaps intrinsically the most interesting; there is always the vague hope that a new school of jazz might develop along such lines, and perhaps the future of British jazz lies in this very direction. Just how far the Brown band, under its new leader Al Fairweather, can go without attacking the basic essentials of the traditional music remains to be seen. It is possible that they too might do nothing more revolutionary than retrace the traditional-mid-period-modern arc. But those of us who are interested to see just where traditional jazz—particularly in the revivalist form—will go from here will be following the fortunes of the band with keen interest.

The advent of skiffle in its British form was completely unforeseen by the prophets, if not by the profiteers. What can happen once can happen again; traditional jazz can give rise to a new form of music altogether, a music which is not jazz but which nevertheless has its roots in jazz. Ken Colyer's experiments with the Omega Brass Band and his attempts to establish a British marching style could spark off such a new music. If we were to bring jazz out into the streets of our towns and cities, reviving the functions and parades which characterised old New Orleans, then jazz might once again develop as a music of the people, moving on perhaps from jazz as we know it to a new and self-contained urban folk-music. Far fetched? Very likely, but it is none the less true that jazz is crying out for renewed recognition as a music of the people rather than a music of musicians. Skiffle itself would seem to have an assured future in this direction, and the fact that British folk-song is being used extensively as raw material, coupled with the fact that skiffle is in essence a music for amateurs, gives some foundation for the belief that a new folk-music of our British towns and cities is not as impossible as we might have thought it a few years ago.

There are three avenues of development, then, within the traditional idiom. New Orleans style will remain to all intents and purposes as a constant; a modern traditionalism is even now co-existing with it and could develop into a distinctive style in its own right; and the possibility of jazz giving birth to a new and living folk-music is, if rather a forlorn hope, by no means an impossible one.

But when we speak about the future of jazz it is, more often than not, the modern product which we have in mind. For modern jazz is expressly and admittedly concerned with the future. The modern jazzman makes no bones about the fact that he is specifically looking for somewhere to go, for new paths to follow and for new worlds to conquer. He aims at pleasing a future-conscious public, and his guiding principle is a sure and solid firm faith in the concept of progress. He tends to form his own private theory of jazz development and to pursue this in his own music, with the result that there are almost as many schools of thought concerning the future of modern jazz as there are modern jazzmen.

It would seem that there are again three broad possibilities, three divergent paths, along any one or more of which the modern music might continue to develop. From many points of view the most logical of these is the path which leads straight back into the main stream of European musical tradition, for it was in this tradition that jazz had some of its roots, and its history during the last forty years may be accurately represented as a slow but progressive rejection of the more powerful Negro influences along with a corresponding accentuation of the legitimate or European factors within its make-up. Thus improvisation has gradually lost more and more ground to the more sophisticated concept of precomposition, and the impromptu balladry of the blues singers has been largely superseded by the professional lyric writer. In the work of such jazz composers as America's John Lewis this trend would seem to be entering its final phase; there are nine parts of European impressionism to every one part of jazz in, for instance, the Modern Jazz Society's version of his "Midsömmer". Indeed, since the early days of the Ellington orchestra the language of jazz has been recognised by both jazz and legitimate musicians as an excellent vehicle for impressionist work.

But whether jazz and the classics can ever effect a stable merger is doubtful, to say the least. One is tempted to ask what such a merger would accomplish, for it would seem that the inevitable end would be the complete swallowing up of jazz within the larger legitimate framework, which is a polite way of saying that jazz would be finished —or modern jazz at least; it is difficult to believe that any such merger would affect or disturb the traditional camp. But if this path is to be pursued, the only alternative to such annihilation is for a line to be drawn at a predetermined stage beyond which even the most progressive jazzman is discouraged from going. But short of obtaining legislation in the Commons—and unless Mr. Dankworth can be persuaded to stand as a progressive independent candidate there doesn't seem very much chance of that—it is difficult to see what practical value such an arbitrarily chosen boundary would have. It would seem, in fact, that this particular path is something of a cul-de-sac, unless we can find a point where it cuts across to another one of our three.

Whatever characteristics modern jazz now shares with the mass of sophisticated music, it must not be forgotten that the two ultimately rest upon quite different foundations. The whole foundation of Western or civilised music lies in the principle of prearranged composition, implying a triple basis of composer, interpreter and consumer, whilst that of jazz lies in the principle of improvised composition wherein composition and interpretation are concurrent acts. The two principles do, of course, overlap; concert music, as we have seen, does not altogether disown improvisation, and modern jazz has quite a strong thread of preconceived arrangement running through it. But basically the two schools of music are resting solidly upon the firm rock of their own choosing. Now, for some hundreds of years the school of precomposition has flourished at the expense of the other, and within it have been produced the operas of Mozart, the symphonies and quartets of Beethoven and the massive worlds of music fashioned by Bruckner and Mahler, and Sibelius and Bartók. But now that, as a result of a fusion of Negro folk-music with the European tradition, a new music has made its entry and developed into what we are calling modern jazz, it is just possible that the virtual monopoly of the precomposition school may be effectively broken. If modern jazz can develop into a new heterophony, reviving the lost art of improvisation and creating a language no less suitable to aesthetic expression than that of "classical" music, any and all deviation from the original non-conformist spirit of New Orleans will be quite justified.

But again it may be that we are aiming our sights too high. It is quite possible that modern jazz may take a third path which leaves it endlessly experimenting merely for the sake of it, and endlessly coughing up new sounds for their own sake. Surely it will not be long before someone plunges into serial technique or quarter-tones or one of the many similar recipes for producing the music of the future? Or again, it could happen that modern jazz will prove, when the whole history of jazz music can be seen in perspective, to be of little more value than the symphonic syncopation of the '20s or the swing of the '30s, all of which we now regard as period music. Time alone will tell, for time is the only sure judge in these matters.

Of one thing we can be sure: in one form or another jazz will continue with us. As the world changes, so jazz will change, but it will still be jazz. It will have its boom periods and its depressions; it will produce its men of genius and its charlatans. Where will jazz go from here? The truth is that there are paths galore, and it will explore them all.

III

BRITISH BANDS TODAY

The Modern Jazz Quartet at the Royal Festival Hall.

BRITISH BANDS TODAY

THE JAZZ COURIERS came into existence on April 7th, 1957, at the Flamingo Club, London, where they have since remained a resident attraction. Founded by co-leaders Ronnie Scott and Tubby Hayes, the group have appeared on both B.B.C. and Independent Television, and toured with the *Daily Express* "package" show, in addition to many sound broadcasts. They have been featured on the same bill as Dave Brubeck.

Personnel: TUBBY HAYES (sax and vibes); RONNIE SCOTT (sax); BILL EYDEN (drums); PHIL BATES (bass); TERRY SHANNON (piano).

MILENBERG JAZZ BAND, formed in 1954 by Jim Shelley. The group first had their headquarters at Walsall Jazz Club and local public-houses. Their efforts, however, met with the disapproval of the local constabulary, and the band moved to Birmingham. There they played the Midland Jazz Club for eighteen months before moving to the Wolverhampton Jazz Club, where they took over from the March Hares. Sessions now held at the George Hotel every Wednesday night. Band's style is traditional.

Personnel: JIM SHELLEY (banjo and leader); JOHNNY GORDON (piano); ALAN BAILEY (clarinet); JOHNNY EVERETT (trumpet); JOHN DICKENSON (trombone); BOB LITTLEWOOD (tuba); BILLIE ORR (vocals).

MIKE PETERS' JAZZ BAND started its professional career with a month's season at a Hamburg night club in February 1957. So successful was this first German date, its returned for another in March of the same year. Boys play "earthy" New Orleans, in the Colyer vein, at the Ken Colyer Club, Newport Street, and Gerry Germain's Club, Croydon. They record for the Dobell-owned "77" label, and have played most of the clubs round London and in the provinces. Called the youngest professional band in the country.

Personnel: MIKE PETERS (trumpet); BARRY CHUM (clarinet); PHIL RHODES (trombone); GRAHAM PATTERSON (piano); REG QUANTRELL (banjo); JOHN RENSHAW (bass); JIM GARFORTH (drums).

KEN COLYER JAZZMEN have the distinction of being led by one of the few musicians in Britain to have played in New Orleans. Ex-seaman Colyer created the Crane River Band, went to New Orleans, and when he returned to London formed the Ken Colyer Band, which was in fact the present Chris Barber Band less Pat Halcox, plus Ken. The current Colyer group, formed in March 1955, rarely tours, but takes over the week-end stand at the Ken Colyer Club in Newport Street. Colyer is credited with leading the revival of archaic New Orleans jazz in Britain.

Personnel: KEN COLYER (trumpet); IAN WHEELER (clarinet); MAC DUNCAN (trombone); JOHN BASTABLE (banjo); ROY FOXLEY (piano); BILL WARD (bass); COLIN BOWDEN (drums).

BRUCE TURNER'S JUMP BAND is renowned for its jump style, based on the early Hodges groups. It has a wide repertoire, including Ellingtonia, Basie, and even "pop" numbers. Formed in the spring of 1947, the band has been voted second (to Dankworth) in the annual *Melody Maker* poll. Leader Turner is rated by many as the country's finest alto player. The group have appeared on television via "6.5 Special", and are resident at the Piccadilly Club, Mondays and Fridays. They record for Nixa. Leader Turner is an ex-Lyttelton and Randall player.

Personnel: BRUCE TURNER (clarinet and alto); TERRY BROWN (trumpet); AL MEAD (piano); BILLY LOCKE (drums); DANNY HAGGERTY (bass).

THE WALLY FAWKES TROGLODYTES: so called because leader Fawkes operates under that name as a cartoonist in the *Daily Mail*. Resident at the Piccadilly Club, twice weekly. Music described as mainstream with traditional instrumentation. Band operates on a semi-professional basis. Whilst band officially records for the Decca label, featured pianist Lennie Felix records independently for Nixa.

Personnel: WALLY FAWKES (clarinet); SPIKE MACKINTOSH (trumpet); JEREMY FRENCH (trombone); RUSS ALLEN (bass); JACKIE TURNER (drums); LENNIE FELIX (featured pianist).

THE MEMPHIS JAZZ BAND was formed in January 1957, members being drawn from the Falkirk Jazz Club. Style is traditional, and although the band hasn't recorded commercially it has cut a few private discs. Local jazz clubs, including the Falkirk Jazz Club, employ the group regularly. In addition, they guest at clubs further afield, such as Dundee.

Personnel: BOB BUSBY (clarinet); CHAS. MALLEY (trumpet and leader); ALEX AMOS (bass); ANGUS MACKAY (tenor and banjo); ART FERGUSSON (drums). Occasionally JIM HARKNESS (trombone).

SECOND CITY JAZZMEN. Banjo-guitarist Stan Keeley, drummer Les Coton, and tuba man Len Bunch, left Birmingham's New Orleans Jazzmen and formed a new band, adhering to no particular style or period of jazz. This was in November 1956, and since then the Second City Jazzmen have become well known all through the Midlands, playing regular dates at the Midland Jazz Club,

Merseysippi and Leicester Clubs. As a result of winning the *Evening Dispatch* band contest, the boys earned an airing on T.V.'s "Bid for Fame". They won, and as a result cut their first record for Esquire in January 1958.

Personnel: BARRY PHILLIPS (trombone); PETE VICARY (piano); LES COTON (drums); LEN BUNCH (tuba); ALAN HEWITT (trumpet and clarinet); JIM HYDE (clarinet); DAVE LEE (clarinet); STAN KEELEY (banjo and electric guitar).

THE DAVE CAREY BAND, formed in January 1956, is composed of veterans and youngsters, forming a happy combination of enthusiasm and experience. Style varies from Dixieland to mainstream. Still semi-professional, the band plays at Streatham Jazz Club. It has a recording contract with Tempo—in fact, it was the first British band to record a long player for this Decca-owned label.

Personnel: DAVE CAREY (drums and vibes); NORMAN HILL (trumpet); DENNIS CROKER (trombone); CYRIL KEEPFER (clarinet); ROY VAUGHAN (piano); ROY MACK (guitar); BOB SINCLAIR (bass).

MICK MULLIGAN BAND. Ex-wine-merchant Mulligan and ex-arts dealer George Melly met back in 1948, and formed an amateur band, with Mick leader and trumpet, George compèring and singing. Considerable success enabled them to turn professional in 1957. Veterans of T.V., radio, and club appearances all over the country, the band specialises in presentation and showmanship. Style best described as "modern traditional". Although mostly working one-nighters in and out of London, the band plays regularly at the Piccadilly Club.

Personnel: MICK MULLIGAN (trumpet); FRANK PARR (trombone); IAN CHRISTIE (clarinet); RONNIE DUFF (tenor); ALAN DUDDINGTON (bass); KEITH APPLEBY (drums); GEORGE MELLY (vocals).

148

SILVER BELL JAZZ BAND was formed early in 1955 at the time of the formation of the Reading County Liberal Jazz Club, where it has since occupied the residency. The band's style can be described as Dixieland-cum-New Orleans. It plays its regular date at the Reading Club on Wednesday evenings. The band has not yet recorded commercially, but recently cut its first private session.

Personnel: CYRIL KENNEDY (trumpet); PETER KEARY (trombone); PHIL COX (drums and alto); DICK SMITH (banjo); BILL LANGDON (bass).

DON RENDELL JAZZ SIX. Led by tenor man Don Rendell, the Six favour what they insist on calling "just jazz". All are composers and arrangers in their own right. The group have toured with the Modern Jazz Quartet. Playing regular dates at the Flamingo Club, it is more often than not kept busy with one-nighters all over the country and occasional trips to the Continent. Recently played in Baden-Baden, and attended the San Remo Festival. Records for both Nixa and Decca labels.

Personnel: DON RENDELL (tenor sax); RONNIE ROSS (baritone and alto); EDDIE HARVEY (trombone); BERT COURTLEY (trumpet); KENNY NAPPER (bass); PHIL SEAMEN (drums).

TOMMY WHITTLE QUINTET, newly formed by tenor leader Whittle, after varied experiments with quartets and big bands. Group play the Mapleton Restaurant's "Club M", and one-nighters in and out of London. Whittle himself went to the States in October 1956, in exchange for Sidney Bechet, and was asked to return again the following April with a Quartet. Most of his jazz work has been recorded with Esquire, and more recently he cut a couple of 78s for the H.M.V. label.

Personnel: TOMMY WHITTLE (lead and tenor); EDDIE THOMPSON (piano); HARRY KLEIN (baritone and alto); MAURICE SALVAT (bass); JACKIE DOUGAN (drums).

AL FAIRWEATHER BAND, hitherto known as the *Sandy Brown Band.* Fairweather, a member of the Brown band for nearly ten years, took over leadership in January 1958. Al has recorded with famed New Orleans clarinet veteran Albert Nicholas on the Danish "Storyville" label, and had his work praised by Kingsley Amis, Steve Race, Humphrey Lyttelton. Band plays Piccadilly Club twice weekly. Although Fairweather has in the past recorded for Columbia, the band will go on recording for the Nixa company.

Personnel: AL FAIRWEATHER (lead, trumpet); TONY MILLINER (trombone); TIMME MANN (bass); WILL HASTIE (clarinet); STAN GREIG (drums); BERT MURRAY (piano).

THE HUMPHREY LYTTELTON BAND, formed in 1948, plays what individualist "Humph" calls "just jazz". Over the past few years chosen to accompany visiting jazz greats Louis Armstrong, Sidney Bechet, Eddie Condon and Jimmy Rushing on their tours of this country. Appears regularly on radio and television. Parlophone handle band's record releases. Biggest seller, "Bad Penny Blues", brought the Lyttelton brand of unstylised music to the attention of the general disc-buying public. Band's London base, the Humphrey Lyttelton Club, 100 Oxford Street, London.

Personnel: HUMPHREY LYTTELTON (trumpet); JIMMY SKIDMORE (tenor sax); TONY COE (clarinet and alto); JOHN PICARD (trombone); IAN ARMIT (piano); BRIAN BROCKLEHURST (bass); EDDIE TAYLOR (drums).

YORKSHIRE JAZZ BAND. Led by tuba-player Bob Barclay, the band was formed in 1948. Leader Barclay runs "Studio 20" in Leeds. The band records for the Esquire label—in all, one L.P., "The War of the Roses", four 78s, and 2 E.P.s. Dick Hawdon, now jazz trumpet with Johnny Dankworth, started his playing career in this band, as did Geoff Sowden, now a traditional band-leader in his own right. Yorkshire brand of music described as "fiery British Trad".

Personnel: BOB BARCLAY (tuba); BERT GAUNT (cornet); ERNIE COOPER (trombone); DENNIS RAYWORTH (clarinet); JACK PAYNE (piano); BRIAN GOLDSBORO (banjo); RONNIE MORRIS (drums).

MERSEYSIPPI JAZZ BAND, formed in 1950, is one of the most original and spirited northern bands, favouring West Coast traditional style. Resident at the Cavern Club, Leeds, personnel has remained stable for years. It sometimes plays the London jazz clubs, but is best known in the North of England. Its records are released by Esquire, and include three L.P.s, a couple of E.P.s, and a number of 78s.

Personnel: PETE DANIELS, JOHN LAWRENCE (trumpets); JOHNNY PARKES (trombone); DON LYDIATT (clarinet); FRANK ROBINSON (piano); KEN BALDWIN (banjo and guitar); DICK GOODWIN (bass); TREVOR CARLISLE (drums).

BRIAN WOOLLEY'S JAZZMEN came together under that name in June 1957, based on an association which goes back to 1953. They have been resident at Leicester Jazz Club since that date, and in August 1957 were offered the residency at Nottingham Jazz Club as well. First London date was in July 1957, since when they have played all the usual haunts, Lyttelton Club, Hot Club of London, Ferry Inn, Chislehurst Caves, etc. In spite of repeated offers, they refuse to turn fully pro. The band's youngest member, drummer John Spooner, who is only 17, is self-taught. Style leans towards Dixieland. First record (Esquire), "Buddy Bolden's Blues", etc., released December 1957.

Personnel: BRIAN WOOLLEY (clarinet); T. C. JONES (cornet); PETE WELLS (trombone); MAURICE COLEMAN (banjo); REG FOSTER (bass); JOHN SPOONER (drums).

ERIC BATTY'S JAZZ ACES, sometimes known as *DIZZY BURTON'S JAZZ ACES,* formed in 1954, based at the Vieux Carré clubs of Manchester and Bolton, tries to get away from the hackneyed "trad." repertoire by using fresh material, Ellingtonia, Creole-influenced tunes, and even suitable current "pops". On hearing the band, veteran New Orleans clarinettist George Lewis said: "You play nearer the style of New Orleans jazz than many of today's Crescent City bands". The group record for Esquire, have two L.P.s, an E.P. and a 78 to their credit.

Personnel: DIZZY BURTON (trumpet); ERIC BATTY (bass); ROY WILLIAMS (trombone); TOM ALKER (clarinet); JIM SMITH (piano); SUE McMANUS (banjo); RON PEACH (drums).

HAPPY WANDERERS STREET BAND. Formed after the war from a group of veteran buskers; average age 50. After years of obscurity finally made national publicity, broadcasts, television. "Voice of America" has played records a number of times on its "Jazz Hour". Style mainly Dixieland; the group play marches, and some "pops". They have two L.P.s, plus a couple of 45s and 78s on release (Esquire). Residency: The Streets of London.

Personnel: BILL LONGMAN (trombone); GEORGE FRANKS (trumpet); VICTOR STAHL, ARTHUR STAHL (banjos); LEONARD STAHL (bass drum).

TERRY LIGHTFOOT BAND made its debut in 1954 on a semi-pro basis, and turned fully professional with two B.B.C. sound broadcasts in October 1956. Its style was New Orleans, its success almost overnight. Since turning pro it has broadcast again, played at N.J.F. concerts, at dances, and appeared on variety tours with George Lewis, The Teenagers vocal group, Freddie Bell and the Bellboys, and Slim Whitman. The band's first record, an E.P., was released in December 1956 on the Nixa label. The same company followed this release with a 78—an experimental disc in that it was the first time the band used a pianist. Although touring continually, the group play regularly at St. Albans Jazz Club.

Personnel: TERRY LIGHTFOOT (clarinet); COLIN SMITH (trumpet); JOHNNY BENNETT (trombone); PADDY LIGHTFOOT (guitar— brother of Terry); COLIN BATES (piano); BILL REID (bass); BILLY LOCKE (drums).

CHRIS BARBER BAND, formed early in 1954, has since become one of the best known in the country as a result of nation-wide one-night stands, Sunday concerts, radio, T.V. and jazz club appearances. Recordings released through Nixa pile up greater sales than any other band in the country. Already on sale: six L.P.s, eight E.P.s and a number of 78s. Most popular record, "Whistlin' Rufus". Late in 1957 the band toured the country with Sister Rosetta Tharpe. Vocalist Ottilie Patterson can be credited with a great deal of the band's popularity.

Personnel: CHRIS BARBER (trombone); MONTY SUNSHINE (clarinet); PAT HALCOX (trumpet); EDDIE SMITH (banjo); DICK SMITH (bass); GRAHAM BURBIDGE (drums); OTTILIE PATTERSON (vocalist).

CY LAURIE BAND came into being back in 1951, and has since built up a fan club of over 14,000 members. Favouring the New

Orleans school of music, leader-founder Cy bases his style on the great Johnnie Dodds. Some of the best traditional musicians in Britain have played in the group, among them Al Fairweather, John Picard, Alan Ellsdon. Boys are resident at their own club, Great Windmill Street, London, each Tuesday, Friday, Saturday and Sunday. Esquire and Melodisc labels release their recordings.

Personnel: CY LAURIE (clarinet); TERRY PITTS (trombone); W. J. RAE (trumpet); TONY RAINE (piano); WAYNE CHANDLER (banjo); STAN LEADER (bass); ERNIE O'MALLEY (drums).

GRAHAM STEWART BAND, a comparatively young group, formed by ex-Cy Laurie trombonist Stewart in November 1956, has already built up a steady following via Wednesday night appearances at the Cy Laurie Club, four 78 records for Decca, and appearances on B.B.C. Television's "6.5 Special". None of the members is over 24 years old. During 1957 Graham was one of the judges at the Moscow Festival of Music.

Personnel: GRAHAM STEWART (trombone); ALAN ELLSDON (trumpet); IAN MCLAREN (clarinet); JIM FOREY (banjo and guitar); ALAN ROOTE (piano); JOHNNY JOHNSON (bass); PETE MAWFORD (drums).

GUS GALBRAITH SEPTET, formed early in 1956 under the name *Original Climax Jazz Band,* was a traditional band playing in New Orleans style. The present highly promising group came on the scene in June 1957 and favour a traditional-cum-mainstream style. Septet can be heard every Saturday night at the Red Lion, Sutton, Surrey, and approximately once a month at the Granada Restaurant in the same town. The band was runner-up in a Mecca "All England Jazz Band Competition" (July 1957) and won outright the "All Surrey Jazz Band Championships" (December 1957), with special commendation for the "adventurous" clarinet and cornet work.

Personnel: GUS GALBRAITH (trumpet); DICK MORRISEY (clarinet); JOHN STERCK (trombone); DOUG CLARK (piano); JOHN EVERSFIELD (guitar); LEON BERNELL (bass); STEVE HARRIS (drums).

DILL JONES TRIO is perhaps the hardest-working small modern group in the country. Since its formation in February 1957, hardly a week has passed without the trio appearing either on radio or television, and sometimes both. Resident at London's El Toro and Marquee clubs. Leader Jones has over the past year become almost as well known as a compère with his own B.B.C. Jazz Club and "What's New?" sound shows. They record for Nixa. Discs include two "Piano Moods" E.P.s and a couple of 78s. The Trio is always called on to accompany Stephane Grapelly on his visits to Britain.

Personnel: DILL JONES (piano); LENNIE BUSH (bass); DANNY CRAIG (drums).

THE JACKSON-BRADSHAW BAND has its headquarters in Accrington, Lancashire. Led by traditionalists Ivor Bradshaw and George Jackson, it has three resident clubs—Accrington (Monday), Blackburn (Friday), Preston (Saturday)—and plays dates at clubs and halls all over the North. Band was formed in June 1956, but has not yet broadcast or recorded commercially. Latest addition to personnel, ex-Black Diamonds (Sheffield) trombonist Norman Jones, who joined the group in January 1958.

Personnel: IVOR BRADSHAW (clarinet and vocal); GEORGE JACKSON (trumpet); NORMAN JONES (trombone); JOHN PARKINSON (banjo); RON WOAN (bass); CED HORNBY (drums and vocal); JACKIE MONTANA (vocalist).

THE TEDDY LAYTON BAND made its debut at a concert in aid of Hungarian Relief at Battersea Town Hall in December 1956, an appearance which led to its first resident job, at the local jazz club. Nowadays semi-resident at Gerry Germain's Jazz Club, Croydon, Croydon Jazz Club, and Luton Jazz Club. Style could best be described as "contemporary New Orleans". Boys recently cut their first disc for Parlophone. Title: "Down by the River".

Personnel: TEDDY LAYTON (clarinet); TREVOR WILLIAMS (trumpet); PETE STRANGE (trombone); BILL COTTON (banjo); JIM GOUDIE (bass); LAURIE CHESCOE (drums).

OWEN BRYCE BAND began under the leadership of trumpet man Bryce in March 1956, who admits to playing "slightly commercial Dixieland". Resident at the Cy Laurie Club each Monday, in addition to regular dates at Maidstone Jazz Club. Although the current band hasn't recorded, Owen himself was in on record sessions when he played with George Webb back in 1946, and later with his Original Dixielanders in 1949 (Decca). Group features quite a few of the members' own compositions, and sometimes divides to form Quartet with clarinet, bass, drums and guitar. The band features blues singer Lynn Trent.

Personnel: OWEN BRYCE (trumpet); JOHNNIE AYRES (clarinet); PETE LONGSDALE (trombone): FRANK SOUTHALL (piano); FRED LEGON (guitar); ALEX O'DWYER (bass); DON ROBB (drums); LYNN TRENT (vocalist).

ALEX WELSH BAND. Scottish-born Alex Welsh made headlines in 1957 when he rejected an offer of trumpet chair in Jack Teagarden's band. Teagarden was not the only visiting American musician to show interest in this young band (formed 1955). Earl Hines said he could get six months' work on the West Coast for a musician of

Welsh's calibre. The band's driving music, derivative of Dixieland jazz, keeps them working non-stop in variety, club dates, recitals and radio. They are signed with Denis Preston for recordings, and appear on the Nixa label.

Personnel: ALEX WELSH (trumpet); ROY CRIMMINS (trombone); FRED HUNT (piano); ARCHIE SEMPLE (clarinet); CHRIS STANTON (bass); JOHN RICHARDSON (drums).

CHRIS MERCER'S IMPERIAL JAZZMEN. The group was formed in Huddersfield in October 1956, and was known as the *Imperial Jazz Band* until April 1957, when leader Chris Mercer took over. After some rehearsal and odd dates, the band began to work in earnest in September 1957, with regular dates in and around Huddersfield. The Jazzmen are now resident at weekly clubs in Huddersfield, Brighouse and Halifax. To date no recordings have been made. Style rather hybrid, but tendency towards classical traditional.

Personnel: CHRIS MERCER (leader and trumpet); NEV FLEETWOOD (clarinet); PETER FOTHERINGHAM (trombone); BOB BLAKE (banjo); TERRY MILLER (bass); JIM DAVIDSON (drums).

WHITE STAR JAZZMEN. The group was formed in August 1957 by Johnny Ashton, who until then had played in both Services and College bands. Originally styled The Maryland Jazzmen—until it was pointed out there was already a band of that name in existence. Music strictly traditional; leader Ashton's policy is to "play what they feel". Band performs at clubs and dances in and around Rotherham, Yorkshire, but hopes to set up a permanent residency during 1958.

Personnel: JOHNNY ASHTON (leader, trumpet and piano); MAURICE THORPE (clarinet); ALAN FINDLAY (trombone); IAN FINDLAY (banjo); MIKE WOODWARD (drums).

TONY KINSEY QUINTET, formed July 1956 by leader-drummer Kinsey when pianist-vibesman Bill le Sage was added as an extension of the already successful Quartet. One of the hardest-working modern groups in the country, resident at London's Flamingo and Florida Clubs. They have represented Britain at the French International Jazz Festivals, at which they have played opposite Gerry Mulligan and Thelonius Monk, as well as the most celebrated Continental musicians. Quintet features a great deal of original material, mostly provided by le Sage. Recordings released through Decca.

Personnel: TONY KINSEY (leader and drums); BILL LE SAGE (vibes and piano); LES CONDON (trumpet); BOB EFFORD (tenor); DAVE Willis (bass).

PARAGON JAZZ BAND made its first appearance on January 9th, 1957, at the Navigation Inn, Derby, but under the name of the *Apex Jazz Band.* The group was slightly re-formed the following April and eventually changed its name to Paragon, with a permanent residency at Derby's Paragon Jazz Club, plus odd dates at charity concerts, etc. Style of jazz played, traditional, with leanings towards Lewis. Recordings have so far only been private.

Personnel: TREVOR ISLAND (leader and trumpet); KEN PRICE (clarinet); TERRY JONES (trombone); BERT MORRIS (piano); ROY HUBBARD (guitar); BARRIE NICOLS (bass); TERRY CARR (drums).

THE DELTA JAZZMEN hail from Burgess Hill, Sussex, and developed out of attempts to form a band within the local Boy Scouts movement. This was early in 1955, but it wasn't until they were joined by Robin Edwards (clarinet) in January 1957 that the group settled down as a sextet, with a leaning towards New Orleans jazz. A year later, however, Robin went to Oxford University and his place was filled by Ted Owen, a young and capable New Orleans stylist. The group plays regularly at the Burgess Hill Jazz Club. No recordings so far.

Personnel: GEORGE H. JONES (trumpet and cornet); ROY LOVE (trombone); TED OWEN (clarinet); MIKE DOE (bass); DEREK BRIDGER (banjo); MIKE FIGG (drums).

THE (NEW) PETER GOLD QUARTET is led by Brighton-born Peter Gold, an enterprising young man who in his twenty-odd years has run a Cool Rhythm Trio, two Quartets, and finally leads both a Quartet and a "band in rehearsal". And all this in spite of considerable local prejudice against jazz in his home town. Quartet plays modern jazz and "standard" pop material, at the Norfolk Hotel, Hot House Club, and Hove Maccabi Youth Club. Pete was encouraged to take up drumming by local pianist Bernie Waterman.

Personnel: PETER GOLD (leader and drums); KEN KNIGHT (piano); JOHNNY STUART (bass); NORMAN GOODALL (tenor); JUDY CARTER (vocals).

THE JAZZ CARDINALS, formed in Huddersfield late in 1955, under the name of *Ed. O'Donnell's Tuxedo Jazz Band.* At this time, the group was led by trombonist O'Donnell, and when he resigned over a disagreement in band policy, and drummer Pete Ridge left to join Mike Peter's Band in London, they were replaced by Derek Wandsworth and Selwyn Hardy, and the group's name changed to the Jazz Cardinals. Leadership was taken over by Keith Smith. The style is New Orleans. Resident clubs: The Parochial Hall, Huddersfield, and the Three Nuns Inn. No commercial recording so far.

Personnel: KEITH SMITH (leader and trumpet); DEREK WANDSWORTH (trombone); BRIAN HODLEY (clarinet); JOHN WATSON (banjo); GEORGE HILL (bass); SELWYN HARDY (drums).

THE JOHNNY DANKWORTH BAND. Certainly the most successful "big band jazz" aggregation in Britain today, led by *Melody Maker* poll-winning altoist Dankworth. Formed October 28th, 1953, played first engagement at the Astoria, Nottingham. Veterans of one-nighters all over the country, the band has not yet played abroad. Because of his views on South African racial problems, leader Dankworth refused the offer of a tour there. Records for Parlophone. Most successful disc so far: "Experiments with Mice", which sold well both here and in the States. Vocalist Cleo Laine voted top female vocalist in Britain.

Personnel: JOHNNY DANKWORTH (leader and alto sax); DERRICK ABBOTT, STAN PALMER, BOB CARSON, COLIN WRIGHT (trumpets); TONY RUSSELL, DANNY ELLWOOD, JACK BOTTERELL, GARY BROWN (trombones); DANNY MOSS (tenor), LAURIE MONK (trombone), DICKIE HAWDON, ALEX LESLIE (baritone saxes); DAVE LEE (piano); ERIC DAWSON (bass); KENNY CLARE (drums); CLEO LAINE (vocalist).

MERCIA JAZZ BAND, formed in October 1952, has its headquarters at Nottingham Rhythm Club on Tuesdays and Fridays. Leader Frank Goodman is the only remaining founder-member of the band, which nevertheless has not had a personnel change since 1955. Fred Pay was active at the very beginning of the jazz revival in this country and in the '40s appeared as solo pianist at the famous Birmingham Town Hall Concerts and Hot Club of London. The band has twice recorded half-hour programmes at club sessions for B.F.N. transmission, and has appeared at the London Lyttelton Club, and major clubs around the country. No records so far. Style strictly traditional.

Personnel: FRANK GOODMAN (leader and clarinet); RAY CRANE, NICK HALLAM (trumpets); ALAN PARKIN (trombone); FRED PAY (piano and vocals); JOHN REID (banjo and guitar); CLAUDE WHITTLE (bass); P. RUSSELL (drums).

THE JOHNNY BECK JAZZ SIX. Formed late in 1957 by alto-clarinettist Beck. Group favours modern "West Coast" school, using quite a few special arrangements by members of the band. The front line were all full-time music students at the Birmingham School of Music before they turned to jazz. Mainly resident at Birmingham's Club Bournebrook and Club '57. No recordings to date.

Personnel: JOHNNY BECK (leader, alto and clarinet); HARRY BURROWS (tenor); ALAN TOMBLIN (trumpet); LES PRICE (piano); VIENCE THOMAS (bass); EDDY HAYNES (drums).

THE NEW ORLEANS JAZZMEN, based at King's Heath, Birmingham, were formed in 1944. Only two of the original members, Pete Rollason and Bobby Pratt, are still with the band, however. Although style leans towards New Orleans, boys try to vary the sound from number to number. Resident at the Adam and Eve, Bradford Street, the Jazzmen play "because they couldn't stop if they tried, and have no ideas of seeking fame and fortune from playing".

Personnel: CHARLES POWELL (trombone and vocals); BOBBY PRATT (trumpet); GEORGE HUXLEY (clarinet and sop. sax); GEORGE WHEELER (banjo); PETE ROLLASON (piano); LEN RUBERY (bass); ROY SAUNDERS (drums).

IV

APPENDICES

APPENDIX 1

EARLY IDEAS ON THE ORIGIN OF THE WORD "JAZZ"

In an attempt to provide an explanation of the origin of the word "jazz", the *Negro Year Book* for 1918 published a statement made by James Reese Europe, "acknowledged King of Jazz", which became the source of much early British (and American) speculation on the subject. Europe credited the name to a dance-combination known as Razz's Band, a group of "truly extraordinary composition. It consisted of a baritone horn, a trombone, a cornet and an instrument made out of the chinaberry tree. This instrument is something like the clarinet and is made by the Southern Negroes themselves. . . . The four musicians of Razz's Band had no idea at all of what they were playing; they improvised [*sic*] as they went along, but such was their innate sense of rhythm that they produced something that was very taking. From the small cafés of New Orleans they graduated to the St. Charles Hotel, and after a time to the Winter Gardens in New York, where they appeared, however, only a few days, the individual musicians being grabbed up by various orchestras in the city. Somehow in the passage of time Razz's Band got changed into Jazz's Band, and from this corruption arose the term 'Jazz'."

Yet more unlikely is the explanation tentatively offered by London's *Dancing Times* in the November 1917 issue, when Negro jazz was still quite unknown in England. The "nigger bands", it was suggested, borrowed the term from the mining camps in the American West, where it was said to be in common use as a slang expression. But of all theories, the most fantastic was that put forward, again by the *Dancing Times* (February 1920), as follows:

"The word 'Dios', which is Portuguese for God, was picked up by English sailors at Indian ports, and when they went to China in the 17th century, they carried the word with them. With the dental softened, this became 'Joss'. The Celestials adopted the word and it was gradually absorbed into their language with a religious meaning such as Joss House, Joss Stick, etc. In San Francisco a Chinese Colony was formed at the beginning of the last century, and as John Chinaman could not bring a Joss Orchestra, he improvised one. The 'Frisco Chinatown Joss Orchestra made a great appeal to the niggers, who improvised again. Now a nigger will say Jazz for Joss. Bands were formed and sent on circuit, and finally Jazz music found its way east to New York and finally to London."

This article was accompanied by a photograph of one such Chinese band over the caption THE ORIGIN OF JAZZ.

Other theories were tame in comparison. Some dragged in the name James or Jas. and Charles or Chas. It is said that "Jasbo" was a greeting used by Negroes, and again that it was the nickname of a popular musician.

Sophie Tucker once claimed to have originated jazz during the First World War, saying that she dropped it when she found that fellow-artistes were cashing in on her brain-child; but whether she claimed credit for coining the name in addition to the music itself is a question that she alone can answer. I imagine that she would pursue neither claim today.

The following extract from the *Musical Mail*, December 1918, provides an excellent example of the reception accorded the earliest so-called jazz to be heard in London:

"Jazz is supposed to have come from America, but from enquiries which have been made, apparently few of our cousins across the pond are prepared to risk their reputation or their lives by admitting any knowledge of it! Like the influenza, this 'frying-pan' music has enveloped us, and seems to be a cross between a boiler factory in full blast and a nursery full of children manipulating the fire-irons during the nurse's absence. There is also what is known as a hydraulic riveter, which can beat a jazz band to a frazzle!

"The composition of the 'band' appears to mainly consist of a hefty and utterly unscrupulous young man who has previously made a tour of the marine stores and collected such curios as frying-pans, tin-lids, fire-irons and such like impedimenta—in fact he is well provided with everything BUT MUSIC! He has neither time, opportunity, knowledge, nor use for *that*. He gathers a few other gentlemen round him who manipulate any instrument which takes their particular fancy, from a banjo and piano to a jew's harp, and they all start level. The aforesaid hefty young man, however, invariably sees them all out—he stays the course with a magnificent disregard for consequences and brings the orgy to a climax and conclusion with a well-directed swipe across the fire-irons with his drum-stick, and a muttered 'That's that!' The audience then reaches for its hat, feels itself all over to be certain nothing is broken, and—flees as one man."

SOME NOTES WITH REFERENCE TO MORALITY AND DANCING

Professor J. WELCH, dancing master, in *Promiscuous Dancing* (1897), apropos the waltz:

"I have watched closely and thought deeply on the subject, and now I have no hesitation in saying that the Waltz is *immoral*. I am happy to say that there still remain numbers of careful fathers who will not allow their daughters to dance it, although a vast proportion of the fashionable and a majority of the middle and lower classes do not seem as yet awakened to its *iniquity*. Dancers of today come in altogether too close contact. In the old time a gentleman merely touched a lady's waist, at the same time holding her right hand in his left. Now he throws his arm clean round her form, *pulls her close to him* as though fearful of losing her, brings his face into actual contact with her soft cheek, and, in a word, hugs her. The Waltz is calculated to do more injury to the young than many of the vices that are preached against from the pulpit and deeply deplored in private life. . . . I have no hesitation in saying that I attribute much of the vice and immorality now prevailing to the insidious influence of the Waltz."

Dancing Times, March 1918, quoting a newspaper (unspecified) on the tango:

"It is not difficult to find the explanation of some of the undesirable dancing. A working man and girl go to a musical comedy. From their stuffy seats high up under the roof, they look down upon the dancers on the stage. These are—so the programme tells them—doing modern ballroom dancing. The man on the stage flings his partner around with apache wildness; she clutches him round the neck, and is swung off her feet. They spin swiftly or undulate slowly across the stage, and the programme calls it a tango. The man and girl go away and talk of these 'ballroom' dances. They try the steps: they are novel and often difficult: they have aroused their interest. The result is that we find scores of young people dancing under the name of 'one-step' or 'tango' the eccentric dances thus elaborated to excite the jaded audiences of a roof-garden or a music-hall. There is no one to tell those young people that they are mistaken in their choice of the steps; that 'society' does not do those dances. They hear hundreds of men and women denouncing the scandalous modern dances, and in their ignorance think that these are the only dances."

Rev. HUGH CHAPMAN, in the *Evening Standard*, March 19th, 1919, on jazz:

"I dined last night at a famous restaurant. Many of the women there were in dresses that reached just above their waists. They were going to a jazz dance."

FRANK SINATRA, 1957, on rock 'n' roll:
". . . this rancid-smelling aphrodisiac. . . ."

APPENDIX 2

JAZZ MAGAZINES

IN the early days of jazz in Britain there were, of course, no jazz magazines. Nor were there any periodicals dealing with subjects of sufficient kinship to give a reasonable picture, even at one remove, of what jazz musicians and enthusiasts were thinking and doing. True, *Dancing Times*, founded in 1910, kept abreast of developments in the field of popular as well as classical dancing, and thus provides some sort of chronicle of events during the pre-jazz "ragtime" age and the years of caricature-jazz that followed it. But no mention was made in its pages of, for instance, the visit of the Original Dixieland Jazz Band, and it was in its pages that "the Jazz" was presented to the public as the latest in a long line of "raggy" dance-steps.

In 1923 the first issues of Sir Compton Mackenzie's *Gramophone* were put on the market. Although primarily slanted in the direction of the "serious music" enthusiast, most of the popular dance records were given at least a mention—and this was a boom period for records, comparable with that of the present day. Under Edgar Jackson the reviews reached a high standard, and even in these days of specialist jazz magazines the *Gramophone* can be relied upon to provide accurate information on, and informed criticism of, the more important issues of each month.

Jazz criticism received its biggest impetus in 1926 when the *Melody Maker* was first published as a monthly magazine. Almost from the start, its policy was one of aggressive evangelism in the cause of the then new "hot jazz". In the first few years the Elizalde brothers were regular contributors, Fred doing almost as much on the printed page as with his band in recommendation of the New York Red Nicholls-

Miff Mole school. In 1930 Spike Hughes, whose Decca-Dents records were proving that America held no monopoly in "hot jazz", took over where Elizalde left off and throughout the '30s he was responsible for record reviews and for a large number of signed articles.

In May 1933 the *Melody Maker* ceased publication as a monthly magazine and became a weekly newspaper. It later experimented in running what was, in effect, a supplementary monthly by taking over *Rhythm*, previously a trade journal circulating among drummers; but this was eventually abandoned and *Rhythm* was incorporated into the weekly *Melody Maker*. Since the war, the paper's policy has been one of fairly popular appeal, and it claims to cover "all modern rhythm music" rather than any narrow jazz field. A particularly useful feature is the weekly diary feature which covers a large cross-section of London and provincial jazz activity.

In 1935 a rival monthly magazine called *Swing Music* was launched. Edited by jazz critic Leonard Hibbs, its coverage was considerably narrower than that of the *Melody Maker*, and after a short period as a quarterly it ceased publication.

The New Orleans revival produced a number of short-lived magazines which contributed little or nothing to the worthwhile literature of jazz. Then in 1950 *Jazz Journal* came to the forefront as the only specialist monthly of the day which successfully pursued a course between the charybdis of popular appeal and the scylla of the arty-crafty esoteric approach. Today it is probably the best jazz periodical published in Britain.

Its younger contemporary, *Jazz Monthly*, follows a similar pattern. It is essential reading for the serious student of the music, but its approach tends to be a little unsmiling and pseudo-intellectual. Its record-reviews, however, are often models in their field. In those of both the *Journal* and the *Monthly*, full discographical data is given.

Jazz Music Mirror is a relative newcomer. Of a fairly popular nature, it has devoted a larger proportion of space to British bands than most of its competitors. *Beat*, another newcomer, is of very limited interest to the enthusiast whose interests lie with the music rather than with the more glamorous of its female exponents.

The New Musical Express is a weekly covering all forms of popular music, including jazz. *Jazz News*, the weekly organ of the National Jazz Federation, covers the whole British field in a fresh, racy style admirably suited to jazz writing.

A large number of American magazines are also obtainable in this country.

THE PRESS

"Jazz is not likely to be continued by decent people," wrote Sir Dyce Duckworth in the *Evening News* of March 18th, 1919. The prophecy is, in many respects, typical of the sort of utterance the Press seized upon when jazz was still a new importation, and when—as was the case with the rock 'n' roll craze of 1957—the slightest story was made the pretext for a front-page splash.

If the popular song and dance industry must be handed the blame for distorting jazz in its British infancy, then the popular Press must take the blame for perpetuating that distortion. Throughout the '20s and '30s a great deal of publicity was given to innumerable facile attacks upon the music: the allegations of immorality—"No decent father would permit his daughter to listen to jazz, let alone dance to it"; of social inferiority—"He said he never listened to jazz (he was the grammar-school type)"; and of trivial comedy—". . . a clarinet solo which was just screamingly funny, more so than anything I have ever heard, even in Duke Ellington". But little was printed in its defence.

Jazz was virtually forgotten by the Press during the war—understandably so. Later, when the New Orleans revival caused the establishment of jazz clubs in Soho and the West End, Fleet Street was quick to associate the music with the hard drinking, gangsterism and drug-trafficking supposedly prevalent in the area.

None of the national newspapers saw in the development of jazz itself an interesting story. None of them noticed the growth of skiffle during 1955 and 1956, until the rock 'n' roll wave made them music-conscious.

However, with a steadily growing stream of books on jazz, and a mounting interest in the music reflected in gramophone record sales figures, newspapers have been forced to toe the line. One of the results is that provincial papers are now willing to report the activities of their local clubs where earlier they would have considered this to mean a lowering of their standards. Writers of the calibre of Iain Lang and Kingsley Amis are being granted space to air their views on current record releases and live events. In short, jazz is treated, if not solemnly, at least sensibly.

One can only hope that a similar revolution may take place in the world of music magazines. A few such do devote a certain amount of space to jazz, but it is generally very small, segregated from the "serious" music and locked away just inside the back cover. But jazz is not seen in true perspective if it is separated from the main stream of music. It is a comi-tragical fact that the people most immersed in musical tradition have been the last to acknowledge the worth of "unspeakable jazz".

APPENDIX 3

BOOKS ON JAZZ

The following list does not include books which deal with jazz as one among many subjects—e.g. general books with a chapter on jazz; nor does it include more than a brief selection of the many biographies and autobiographies of musicians. Books that are for reference only are not included.

As is to be expected, the emphasis in all these books is on American jazz.

Dates given are those of first publication in Britain.

Year	Author	Title	Publisher
1927	R. W. S. Mendl	*The Appeal of Jazz*	Phillip Allan
1934	S. R. Nelson	*All About Jazz*	Cranston
1936	Louis Armstrong	*Swing That Music*	Longmans
	Hugues Panassié	*Hot Jazz*	Cassell
1940	W. Hobson	*American Jazz Music*	Dent
1945	D. S. Enefer	*Jazz in Black and White*	Alliance Press
	Larry Stave	*Fashions in Jazz*	Bear Hudson
	K. Williamson	*Jazz Quiz*	Durban
1947	Paul Arundel	*This Swing Business*	Arthur Unwin
	Iain Lang	*Jazz in Perspective: the Background of the Blues*	Hutchinson
	A. McCarthy (ed.)	*Jazzbook 1947*	Editions Poetry
	Milton Mezz Mezzrow	*Really the Blues*	Musician's Press
	George S. Rosenthal Frank Zachary Fredk. Ramsay, Jnr. Rudi Blesh	*Jazzways*	Museum Press
	K. Williamson	*Rhythm Digest*	Panda Publications

1948	Eddie Condon ⎫ Thomas Sugrue ⎬	*We Called It Music*	Peter Davies
1949	Rudi Blesh	*Shining Trumpets*	Cassell
1952	Rex Harris Alan Lomax	*Jazz* *Mister Jelly Roll*	Penguin Books Cassell
1954	D. S. Enefer Humphrey Lyttelton	*Daily Dispatch Jazz Book* *I Play as I Please*	Daily Dispatch MacGibbon & Kee
1955	Louis Armstrong	*Satchmo: My Life in New Orleans*	Peter Davies
	A. McCarthy (ed.)	*Jazzbook 1955*	Cassell
	Nat Shapiro ⎫ Nat Hentoff ⎬ (eds.)	*Hear Me Talkin' To Ya*	Peter Davies
1956	André Hodeir	*Jazz: its Evolution and Essence*	Secker & Warburg
	Alun Morgan ⎫ Raymond Horricks ⎬	*Modern Jazz, a Survey of Developments Since 1939*	Gollancz
1957	W. C. Handy	*Father of the Blues*	Sidgwick & Jackson
	Fredk. Ramsay, Jnr. ⎫ Charles Edward Smith ⎬	*Jazzmen*	Sidgwick & Jackson
	Marshall Stearns	*The Story of Jazz*	Sidgwick & Jackson
	Sinclair Traill ⎫ Gerald Lascelles ⎬ (eds.)	*Just Jazz*	Peter Davies
	Michael Wyler	*A Glimpse at the Past*	Jazz Publications
	Elliot Paul Sinclair Traill (ed.)	*That Crazy Music* *Concerning Jazz*	Muller Faber

A SELECTED DISCOGRAPHY

PART ONE

American music that has had a pronounced effect on British jazz.

Abbreviations used in the Discography

as	Alto sax	pa	Piano accordion
bj	Banjo	p	Piano
bs	Bass	ss	Soprano sax
bts	Baritone sax	tb	Trombone
cl	Clarinet	tp	Trumpet
co	Cornet	ts	Tenor sax
ds	Drums	tu	Tuba
fl	Flute	vn	Violin
g	Guitar	vo	Vocal
	wb	Washboard	

Original Dixieland Jazz Band in New York　　　H.M.V. DLP 1065

Dixie Jazz Band	*Feb. 24th 1917*
Livery Stable Blues	*do.*
Skeleton Jangle	*March 25th 1918*
Tiger Rag	*do.*
Sensation Rag	*June 25th 1918*
Bluin' the Blues	*Aug. 17th 1918*
Mournin' Blues	*do.*
Clarinet Marmalade	*do.*

Personnel: Nick la Rocca (co) Larry Shields (cl) Eddie Edwards (tb) Harry Ragas (p) Tony Sbarbaro (ds).

Original Dixieland Jazz Band in London　　　COL. 33S 1087

At the Jazz Band Ball	*April 16th 1919*
Ostrich Walk	*May 19th 1919*
Tell Me	*Jan. 1st 1920*
Lasses' Candy	*do.*

Satanic Blues	*Aug. 19th 1920*
Mammy o' Mine	*Jan. 1st 1920*
Look at 'em Doing It	*May 19th 1920*
I've Lost My Heart in Dixieland	*Jan. 1st 1920*

Personnel: Nick la Rocca (co) Larry Shields (cl) Emil Christian (tb) Billy Jones (p) Tony Sbarbaro (ds).

Bix Beiderbecke and the Wolverine Orchestra   LONDON AL 3532

(A)	Fidgety Feet	*Feb. 18th 1924*
(A)	Jazz Me Blues	*do.*
(B)	Oh, Baby	*May 16th 1924*
(B)	Copenhagen	*do.*
(B)	Riverboat Shuffle	*do.*
(C)	Sensation Rag	*Sept. 16th 1924*
(C)	Lazy Daddy (2 versions)	*do.*

Personnel:
(*A*) Bix Beiderbecke (co) Al Gande (tb) Jimmy Hartwell (cl) George Johnson (ts) Dick Voynow (p) Bob Gillette (bj) Min Leibrook (tu) Vic Moore (ds).
(*B*) As (*A*), without Al Gande.
(*C*) As (*A*), with George Brunis (tb) added.

Original Memphis Five   LONDON AL 3541

Jelly Roll Blues
The Great White Way Blues
Bunch of Blues
Shufflin' Mose
} *exact dates not known*

Personnel: Phil Napoleon (tp) Miff Mole (tb) Jimmy Lytell (cl) Frank Signorelli (p) Jack Roth (ds).

Red and Miff's Stompers

Stampede
Alabama Stomp
Black Bottom Stomp
Hurricane
} *exact dates not known*

Personnel: Red Nicholls (co) Miff Mole (tb) Jimmy Dorsey (cl & as) Arthur Schutt (p) Vic Berton (ds).

M   177

Louis Armstrong's Hot Five (and Seven)   COL. 33S 1007

    (*A*)   Struttin' With Some Barbecue   *Dec. 9th 1927*
    (*B*)   Squeeze Me   *June 29th 1928*
    (*B*)   Don't Jive Me   *June 28th 1928*
    (*C*)   Basin Street Blues   *Dec. 4th 1928*
    (*D*)   That's When I'll Come Back   *May 14th 1927*
    (*D*)   Potato Head Blues   *May 10th 1927*
    (*D*)   Melancholy Blues   *May 11th 1927*
    (*E*)   Tight Like This   *Dec. 12th 1928*

Personnel:

(*A*) Louis Armstrong (co) Johnny Dodds (cl) Edward "Kid" Ory (tb) Johnny St. Cyr (bj).

(*B*) Louis Armstrong (co) Jimmy Strong (cl & ts) Fred Robinson (tb) Earl Hines (p) Mancy Cara (bj) Zutty Singleton (ds).

(*C*) As (*B*), with Earl Hines also playing celeste.

(*D*) Louis Armstrong (co) Johnny Dodds (cl) Edward "Kid" Ory (tb) Lil Armstrong (p) Johnny St. Cyr (bj) Pete Briggs (tu) Warren "Baby" Dodds (ds).

(*E*) As (*B*), with Don Redman (as).

Duke Ellington and his Famous Orchestra   VOGUE-CORAL LRA 10028

    (*A*)   Yellow Dog Blues   *June 5th 1928*
    (*A*)   Tishomingo Blues   *do.*
    (*B*)   Awful Sad   *Oct. 20th 1928*
    (*C*)   Tiger Rag   *Jan. 8th 1929*
    (*D*)   Jazz Convulsions   *Sept. 13th 1929*
    (*D*)   Creole Rhapsody   *Jan. 20th 1931*

Personnel:

(*A*) Duke Ellington (p) Bubber Miley, Louis Metcalfe, Arthur Whetsel (tps) Joe Nanton (tb) Johnny Hodges (as & ss) Harry Carney (as & bts) Barney Bigard (cl & ts) Fred Guy (bj) Wellman Braud (bs) Sonny Greer (ds).

(*B*) As (*A*), without Louis Metcalfe.

(*C*) Duke Ellington (p) Bubber Miley, Arthur Whetsel, Freddy Jenkins (tps) Joe Nanton (tb) Johnny Hodges (as & ss) Barney Bigard (cl & ts) Harry Carney (cl, as & bts) Fred Guy (bj) Wellman Braud (bs) Sonny Greer (ds).

(*D*) Duke Ellington (p) Cootie Williams, Arthur Whetsel, Freddie Jenkins (tps) Joe Nanton, Juan Tizol (tbs) Johnny Hodges (as & ss) Barney Bigard (cl & ts) Harry Carney (cl, as & bts) Fred Guy (bj) Wellman Braud (bs) Sonny Greer (ds).

Spike Hughes and his All American Orchestra   DECCA LK 4173

(A)	Nocturne	*April 18th 1933*
(A)	Pastoral	*do.*
(B)	Bugle Call Rag	*do.*
(C)	Arabesque	*May 18th 1933*
(C)	Fanfare	*do.*
(C)	Sweet Sorrow Blues	*do.*
(C)	Music at Midnight	*do.*
(D)	Sweet Sue	*May 19th 1933*
(E)	Air in D Flat	*do.*
(E)	Donegal Cradle Song	*do.*
(E)	Firebird	*do.*
(D)	How Come You Do Me Like You Do?	*do.*

Personnel (Spike Hughes directing throughout):

(*A*) Benny Carter, Wayman Carver, Howard Johnson (as) Coleman Hawkins (ts) Shad Collins, Leonard Davis, Bill Dillard (tps) Wilbur de Paris, Dicky Wells, George Washington (tbs) Nicholas Rodriguez (p) Lawrence Lucie (g) Ernest Hill (bs) Kaiser Marshall (ds).

(*B*) As (*A*), except Sid Catlett (ds) replaces Kaiser Marshall.

(*C*) Benny Carter (as & cl) Wayman Carver (as & fl) Howard Johnson (as) Leon "Chu" Berry, Coleman Hawkins (ts) Henry Allen, Leonard Davis, Bill Dillard (tps) Wilbur de Paris, Dicky Wells, George Washington (tbs) Luis Russell (p) Lawrence Lucie (g) Ernest Hill (bs) Kaiser Marshall (ds).

(*D*) Benny Carter (as) Wayman Carver (fl) Leon "Chu" Berry, Coleman Hawkins (ts) Henry Allen (tp) Dicky Wells (tb) Nicholas Rodriguez (p) Lawrence Lucie (g) Spike Hughes (bs) Sid Catlett (ds).

(*E*) As (*C*), except Benny Carter plays ss and Nicholas Rodriguez (p) replaces Luis Russell.

King Oliver's Creole Jazz Band   LONDON AL 3504

Chimes Blues
Froggie Moore
Just Gone
Canal Street Blues
Dipper Mouth Blues } *March and April 1923*
Weather Bird Rag
Mandy Lee Blues
Snake Rag

Personnel: Joe "King" Oliver, Louis Armstrong (cos) Honoré Dutray (tb) Johnny Dodds (cl) Lil Hardin (p) Bill Johnson (bj) Warren "Baby" Dodds (ds).

Benny Goodman Jazz Concert   PHILIPS BBL 7010

Let's Dance (Orch.)
Ridin' High (Orch.)
Nice Work if You Can Get It (Trio)
Vibraphone Blues (Quart.)
Sheik of Araby (Quart.)
Peckin' (Orch.)
Sunny Disposish (Orch.)
Nagasaki (Quart.)   *These performances*
St. Louis Blues (Orch.)   *were all recorded*
Clarinet Marmalade (Orch.)   *from radio broadcasts*
Time on My Hands (Trio)   *during 1937-38, the*
Stardust (Orch.)   *exact dates of which*
Benny Sends Me (Quart.)   *are not available.*
Everybody Loves My Baby (Quart.)
Josephine (Orch.)
Killer Diller (Quart.)
Someday, Sweetheart (Orch.)
Caravan (Orch.)
Goodbye (Orch.)

Personnel: Benny Goodman (cl) Harry James, Ziggy Elman, Chris Griffin (tps) Red Ballard, Vernon Brown, Murray McEachern (tbs) Hymie Shertzer, Babe Russin, Vido Musso, George Koenig, Art Rollini (saxes) Jess Stacy, Teddy Wilson (ps) Harry Goodman (bs) Allan Reuss (g) Gene Krupa (ds).

"Fats" Waller Favourites   H.M.V. DLP 1008

(A)	Honeysuckle Rose	May 13th 1941
(A)	Ain't Misbehavin'	Aug. 2nd 1929
(B)	I Can't Give You Anything But Love	Nov. 3rd 1939
(C)	Two Sleepy People	Oct. 13th 1938
(D)	Minor Drag	March 1st 1929
(E)	The Joint Is Jumpin'	Oct. 7th 1937
(C)	Hold Tight	Jan. 19th 1939
(F)	Your Feet's Too Big	Nov. 3rd 1939

Personnel:

(*A*) Thomas "Fats" Waller (p).

(*B*) Thomas "Fats" Waller (p & vo) Herman Autry (tp) Chauncey Graham (ts) John Smith (g) Cedric Wallace (bs) Larry Hinton (ds) Una Mae Carlisle (vo).

(*C*) Thomas "Fats" Waller (p & vo) Herman Autry (tp) Gene Sedric (cl & ts) Al Casey (g) Cedric Wallace (bs) Slick Jones (ds).

(*D*) Thomas "Fats" Waller (p) Charlie Gains (tp) Charlie Irvis (tb) Arville Harris (cl & as) Eddie Condon (bj).

(*E*) As (*C*), except Charles Turner (bs) replaces Cedric Wallace.

(*F*) As (*B*), without Una Mae Carlisle.

Louis Armstrong and his Orchestra BRUNSWICK LA 8528

(*A*)	Mahogany Hall Stomp	Oct. 3rd 1935
(*B*)	Dipper Mouth Blues	Aug. 7th 1936
(*C*)	When The Saints Go Marching In	May 13th 1938
(*D*)	Save It, Pretty Mama	April 5th 1939
(*D*)	West End Blues	do.
(*E*)	Bye and Bye	Dec. 18th 1939
(*F*)	When It's Sleepy Time Down South	Nov. 16th 1941
(*F*)	You Rascal, You	do.

Personnel:

(*A*) Louis Armstrong, Leonard Davis, Gus Aitkin, Louis Bacon (tps) Harry White, James Archey (tbs) Henry Jones, Charlie Holmes (as) Bingie Madison, Greely Walton (ts) Luis Russell (p) Lee Blair (g) "Pops" Foster (bs) Paul Barbarin (ds).

(*B*) Louis Armstrong, George Thow, "Toots" Camarata (tps) Bobby Byrne, Joe Yukl, Don Mattison (tbs) Jimmy Dorsey (cl & as) Jack Stacey (as) Fud Livingstone, Skeets Herfurt (ts) Bobby Van Epps (p) Roscoe Hillman (g) Jim Taft (bs) Ray McKinley (ds).

(*C*) Louis Armstrong, Shelton Hemphill (tps) J. C. Higginbotham (tb) Charlie Holmes, Rupert Cole (as) Bingie Madison (cl & ts) Luis Russell (p) Lee Blair (g) "Pops" Foster (bs) Paul Barbarin (ds).

(*D*) Louis Armstrong, Shelton Hemphill, Otis Johnson, Henry Allen (tps) Wilbur de Paris, George Washington, J. C. Higginbotham (tbs) Charlie Holmes, Rupert Cole (as) Bingie Madison, Joe Garland (ts) Luis Russell (p) Lee Blair (g) "Pops" Foster (bs) Sid Catlett (ds).

(*E*) As (*D*), except that Bernard Flood (tp) replaces Otis Johnson.

(*F*) Louis Armstrong (tp & vo) Shelton Hemphill, Gene Prince, Frank Galbraith (tps) George Washington, Norman Greene, Henderson Chambers (tbs) Rupert Cole, Carl Frye (as) Prince Robinson, Joe Garland (ts) Luis Russell (p) Lawrence Lucie (g) Hayes Alvis (bs) Sid Catlett (ds).

"Jelly Roll" Morton's Red Hot Peppers H.M.V. DLP 1071

(*A*)	Black Bottom Stomp	Sept. 15th 1926
(*B*)	Sidewalk Blues	Sept. 21st 1926
(*C*)	Beale Street Blues	June 10th 1927
(*A*)	Grandpa's Spells	Dec. 16th 1926

(B) Dead Man Blues   *Sept. 21st 1926*
(B) Steamboat Stomp   *do.*
(B) Cannon Ball Blues   *Dec. 16th 1926*
(C) The Pearls   *June 10th 1927*
(A) Smoke-House Blues   *Sept 15th 1926*
(C) Wild Man Blues   *June 4th 1927*

Personnel:
(A) George Mitchell (co) Edward "Kid" Ory (tb) Omer Simeon (cl) Ferdinand "Jelly Roll" Morton (p) Johnny St. Cyr (bj) John Lindsay (bs) Andrew Hilaire (ds).

(B) As (A), with Barney Bigard and Darnell Howard (cls) and unknown 2nd co.

(C) George Mitchell (co) Gerald Reeves (tb) Johnny Dodds (cl) "Stump" Evans (as) Ferdinand "Jelly Roll" Morton (p) Arthur "Bud" Scott (g) Quinn Wilson (tu) Warren "Baby" Dodds (ds).

Louis Armstrong and his All-Stars   H.M.V. DLP 1015

Rockin' Chair
Ain't Misbehavin'
Back o' Town Blues
St. James Infirmary   } *April 24th 1947*
Pennies From Heaven
Save It, Pretty Mama

Personnel: Louis Armstrong, Bobby Hackett (tps) Jack Teagarden (tb) Michael "Peanuts" Hucko (cl & ts) Dick Cary (p) Bob Haggart (bs) Sid Catlett, George Wettling (alternative ds).

Dizzy Gillespie and his Orchestra   VOGUE LDE 076

Emanon
Ool-Ya-Koo
Stay On It
Good Bait   } *May 1949*
One Bass Hit
Manteca

Personnel: John "Dizzy" Gillespie (tp) Joe Brown, Joe Gayles, Ernie Henry, James Moodie, Cecil Payne (saxes) Dave Brown, Willie Cook, Elman Wright (tps) Andy Duryea, William Sheppard, Jess Tarrant (tbs) James Fareman (p) Nelson Boyd (bs) Teddy Stewart (ds) Chano Pozo (bongoes, conga drum).

Louis Armstrong and his All-Stars   DECCA LAT 8084

When It's Sleepy Time Down South ⎫
Jeepers Creepers
Tin Roof Blues
Bucket's Got a Hole in It
Rose Room
Brother Bill
Lazy River   ⎬   *Jan. 21st 1955*
'Tain't What You Do
Perdido
Blues for Bass
Don't Fence Me In
Stompin' at the Savoy   ⎭

Personnel: Louis Armstrong (tp) Barney Bigard (cl) Trummy Young (tb)
Billy Kyle (p) Arvell Shaw (bs) Barrett Deems (ds) Velma Middleton (vo).

Duke Ellington and his Orchestra   DECCA LTZ-N 15029

East St. Louis Toodle-oo ⎫
Creole Love Call
Stompy Jones
The Jeep Is Jumpin'
Jack the Bear
In a Mellow Tone
Ko-Ko   ⎬   *Feb. 7th and 8th 1956*
Midriff
Stomp, Look and Listen
Unbooted Character
Lonesome Lullaby
Upper Manhattan Medical Group ⎭

Personnel: Duke Ellington (p) Cat Anderson, Clark Terry, Willie Cook
(tps) Ray Nance (tp & vn) Britt Woodman, John Sanders, Quentin
Jackson (tbs) Johnny Hodges (as) Russell Procope (as & cl) Paul Gonsalves
(ts) Jimmy Hamilton (ts & cl) Harry Carney (bass-cl & bts) Jimmy Woode
(bs) Sam Woodyard (ds).

Modern Jazz Quartet   ESQUIRE 20-038

Django   *Dec. 23rd 1954*
One Bass Hit   *do.*
Milano   *do.*
La Ronde   *Jan. 9th 1955*

Personnel: John Lewis (p) Milt Jackson (vibes) Percy Heath (bs) Kenny
Clarke (ds).

Count Basie and his Orchestra　　　　　　　　COLUMBIA 33CX 10026

Alright, O.K., You Win
The Comeback
Send Me Someone To Love
Ev'ry Day
In the Evening　　　　　　} *1955*
My Baby Upsets Me
Teach Me Tonight
Roll 'em Pete
Every Day I Have the Blues

Personnel uncertain, but probably: William "Count" Basie (p) Bill Graham, Marshall Royal (as) Frank Foster, Frank Wess (ts) Charlie Fowlkes (bts) Ed Culley, Renauld Jones, Thad Jones, Joe Newman (tps) Henry Coker, Bill Hughes, Benny Powell (tbs) Freddy Green (g) Eddie Jones (bs) Sonny Payne (ds) Joe Williams (vo).

PART TWO

A representative selection of British jazz records.

Chris Barber's Jazz Band　　　　　　　　DECCA LF 1198

(*A*) Bobby Shaftoe
(*A*) New Orleans Blues
(*A*) Chimes Blues
(*A*) Merrydown Rag
(*A*) The Martinique　　　　　} *July 13th 1954*
(*A*) Stevedore Stomp
(*B*) Rock Island Line } *Lonnie Donegan's*
(*B*) John Henry　　　　 *Skiffle Group*

Personnel:

(*A*) Pat Halcox (co) Chris Barber (tb) Monty Sunshine (cl) Lonnie Donegan (bj) Jim Bray (bs) Ron Bowden (ds).

(*B*) Lonnie Donegan (g & vo) Chris Barber (bs) Beryl Bryden (wb).

184

Chris Barber's Jazz Band   JAZZ TODAY NJL I

   (A) Doin' the Crazy Walk   *Sept. 16th 1955*
   (A) Baby   *do.*
   (A) Magnolia's Wedding Day   *Sept. 25th 1955*
   (A) Dixie Cinderella   *do.*
   (B) New St. Louis Blues   *do.*
   (A) Here Comes My Blackbird   *Sept. 1st 1955*
   (C) Can't We Get Together   *Sept. 16th 1955*
   (B) I Can't Give You Anything But Love   *do.*
   (A) Sweet Savannah Sue   *Sept. 29th 1955*
   (A) Porgy   *do.*
   (D) Diga Diga Doo   *Jan. 13th 1955*

Personnel:

(A) Chris Barber (tb) Monty Sunshine (cl) Pat Halcox (co) Lonnie Donegan
    (bj) Mickey Ashman (bs) Ron Bowden (ds).

(B) As (A), with Ottilie Patterson (vo).

(C) As (A), without Lonnie Donegan.

(D) As (A), except Jim Bray (bs) replaces Micky Ashman.

Fawkes-Turner Sextet   DECCA DFE 6192

Fishmouth
Summertime   *Aug. 3rd 1954*
My Monday Date

Personnel: Wally Fawkes (cl) Bruce Turner (as) Johnny Parker (p) Freddy
Legon (g) Mickey Ashman (bs) Ron Bowden (ds).

Sandy Brown's Jazz Band   TEMPO TAP 3

   (A) Nobody Met the Train
   (A) Stay
   (B) Swiss Kriss
   (C) High Time
   (D) Look the Other Way   *May 27th 1956*
   (E) (B) Candy Stripes
   (F)   My Neck of the Woods
   (G) Mouseparty

Personnel: Sandy Brown (cl) Al Fairweather (tp) John R. T. Davies (tb)
Alan Thomas (p) Mo Umansky (bj) Brian Parker (bs) Graham Burbage (ds).

Also, as guest stars:

(A) William Disley (g); (B) Stan Greig (ds); (C) Spike Macintosh (tp);
(D) Johnny Pickard (tp); (E) Dave Stevens (p); (F) Dick Heckstall-Smith
(ss); Bob Clarke (vn).

Sandy Brown's Jazz Band   JAZZ TODAY NJL 9

Go Ghana ⎤
Scales ⎥
The Card ⎥
Monochrome ⎥
Those Blues ⎥ *March 5th 1957*
Wild Life ⎥
Doctor Blues, I Presume ⎥
Ognoliya ⎥
Saved By The Blues ⎦

Personnel: Sandy Brown (cl) Al Fairweather (tp) Jeremy French (tb)
Ian Armit (p) William Disley (g & bj) Tim Mahn (bs) Graham Burbridge
(ds).

Ken Colyer's Jazzmen   DECCA LF 1152

Goin' Home ⎤
Stockyard Strut ⎥
Isle of Capri ⎥
Cataract Rag ⎥ *Nov. 4th 1953*
Harlem Rag ⎥
Early Hours ⎥
La Harpe Street ⎥
Too Busy ⎦

Personnel: Ken Colyer (tp) Monty Sunshine (cl) Chris Barber (tb) Lonnie
Donegan (bj) Jim Bray (bs) Ron Bowden (ds).

Ken Colyer's Jazzmen and Skiffle Group   DECCA LF 1196

(A)	Sing On	*Sept. 9th 1954*
(A)	Lord, Lord, Lord	*do.*
(A)	Faraway Blues	*do.*
(A)	Moose March	*do.*
(B)	Midnight Special	*June 25th 1954*
(B)	Casey Jones	*do.*
(B)	K. C. Moan	*do.*
(A)	Saturday Night Function	*Sept. 9th 1954*
(A)	Shim-me-sha Wabble	*do.*

Personnel:

(A) Ken Colyer (tp) Bernard Bilk (cl) Ed O'Donnell (tb) William Disley (bj)
Dick Smith (bs) Stan Greig (ds).

(B) Ken Colyer (g) Alexis Korner (g & mandolin) Mickey Ashman (bs)
Bill Colyer (wb).

Ottilie Patterson with Chris Barber's Jazz Band   JAZZ TODAY JTE 102

Trouble in Mind	*March 8th 1955*
Pallet on the Floor	*do.*
Sister Kate	*March 9th 1955*
Poor Man's Blues	*March 3rd 1955*

Personnel: Ottilie Patterson (vo) Chris Barber (tb) Pat Halcox (tp) Monty Sunshine (cl) Lonnie Donegan (bj) Jim Bray (bs) Ron Bowden (ds).

Cy Laurie's Jazz Band   ESQUIRE 32-008

Jazzin' Baby Blues
Canal Street Blues
Don't Forget to Mess Around
Flat Foot
Where Did You Stay Last Night? } *March 26th 1954*
All the Girls
Runnin' Wild
Milenburg Joys
Ice Cream

Personnel: Al Fairweather (tp) Johnny Pickard (tb) Cy Laurie (cl) Alan Thomas (p) Johnny Potter (bj) Dave Wood (bs) Ron McKay (ds).

Humphrey Lyttelton's Jazz Band   PARLOPHONE PMC 1012

Texas Moaner
Coal Black Shine
Last Smile Blues
Elephant Stomp
Wally Plays The Blues
My Bucket's Got a Hole in It } *Sept. 2nd 1954*
I Double Dare You
That's The Blues, Old Man
Feline Stomp
St. James Infirmary
Memphis Shake
Mo Pas Lemme Ca

Personnel: Humphrey Lyttelton (tp) Wally Fawkes (cl) Bruce Turner (as & ss) Johnny Parker (p) Freddy Legon (bj & g) Mickey Ashman (bs) George Hopkinson (ds).

Humphrey Lyttelton and his Band   PARLOPHONE GEP 8514

(*A*) Ace in the Hole   *Feb. 15th 1950*
(*B*) Coffee Grinder   *July 19th 1950*
(*C*) Snag It   *Dec. 2nd 1954*
(*D*) Careless Love Blues   *do.*

Personnel:

(*A*) Humphrey Lyttelton (co) Wally Fawkes, Ian Christie (cls) Keith Christie (tb) George Webb (p) Buddy Vallis (bj) John Wright (bs) George Hopkinson (ds).

(*B*) As (*A*), except Mickey Ashman (bs) replaces John Wright.

(*C*) Humphrey Lyttelton (tp) Wally Fawkes (cl) Bruce Turner (as) John Picard (tb) Johnny Parker (p) Freddy Legon (bj) Mickey Ashman (bs) George Hopkinson (ds).

(*D*) As (*C*), except Freddy Legon plays guitar.

George Chisholm Sextet   DECCA LK 4147

(*A*) Makin' Whoopee   *March 29th 1956*
(*A*) I Gotta Right to Sing The Blues   *do.*
(*B*) Needle-Noodle-Noo   *April 6th 1956*
(*C*) Sonny Boy   *May 14th 1956*
(*D*) Lazy River   *March 23rd 1956*
(*B*) Just You Just Me   *April 6th 1956*
(*D*) 'Deed I Do   *March 23rd 1956*
(*A*) Georgetta   *March 29th 1956*
(*C*) When Your Lover Has Gone   *May 14th 1956*
(*C*) Weekend Male   *do.*
(*D*) Blues For Twos   *March 23rd 1956*
(*C*) I May Be Wrong   *May 14th 1956*

Personnel:

(*A*) George Chisholm (tb) Joe Harriott (as) Bob Burns (ts & cl) Harry Klein (bs) Max Harris (p) Joe Muddel (bs) Phil Seamen (ds) Jack Llewellyn (g).

(*B*) George Chisholm (tb) Bob Burns (ts) Max Harris (p) Ike Isaacs (g) Joe Muddel (bs) Phil Seamen (ds).

(*C*) George Chisholm (tb) Bob Burns (as) Derek Collins (ts) Ken Goldie (tu) Bill le Sage (vibes) Max Harris (p) Joe Muddel (bs) Phil Seamen (ds).

(*D*) George Chisholm (tb) Bertie King (as) Derek Collins (ts) Ken Goldie (tu) Alan Clare (p) Ike Isaacs (g) Joe Muddel (bs) Phil Seamen (ds).

Dill Jones Trio   NIXA NJE 1024

Viper's Drag
Blues for an Ancient Virginal } *Sept. 7th 1956*
Moonglow
'Deed I Do

Personnel: Dill Jones (p) Major Holley (bs) Phil Seamen (ds).

Johnny Dankworth Orchestra   PARLOPHONE PMC 1043

(A)   Export Blues   *Aug. 29th 1957*
(A)   Just a-Sittin' and a-Rockin'   *do.*
(A)   Somebody Loves Me   *do.*
(A)   Hullabaloo   *do.*
(A)   Stompin' at the Savoy   *do.*
(B)   Limehouse Blues   *March 21st 1957*

Personnel:

(A) Johnny Dankworth (as) Danny Moss (ts) Alex Leslie (bts & cl) Dickie
    Hawdon (tp) Laurie Monk (tb) Derrick Abbott, Stan Palmer, Colin
    Wright, Bert Courtley (secondary tps) Jack Botterell, Garry Brown,
    Danny Elwood, Tony Russell (secondary tbs) Dave Lee (p) Eric
    Dawson (bs) Kenny Clare (ds).
(B) As (A), except Tommy Whittle (ts) replaces Danny Moss and Bill
    Metcalfe (tp) replaces Bert Courtley.

Laurie Monk Quartet

Somerset Morn } *Sept. 4th 1957*
Horoscope

Personnel: Laurie Monk (tb) Johnny Dankworth (as) Eric Dawson (bs)
Kenny Clare (ds).

Dickie Hawdon Quintet

One For Janet } *March 25th 1957*
Magenta Midget

Personnel: Dickie Hawdon (tp) Johnny Dankworth (as) Dave Lee (p)
Eric Dawson (bs) Kenny Clare (ds).

Victor Feldman Modern Jazz Quartet   ESQUIRE EP 35

Monsoon ⎱ *Dec. 14th 1954*
What Goes? ⎰

Personnel: Victor Feldman (vibes & conga drum) Tommy Pollard (p)
Lennie Bush (bs) Phil Seamen (ds).

Kenny Graham's Afro-Cubists with Victor Feldman   ESQUIRE 20-064

Mogambo ⎫
Keep Happy ⎬ *Sept. 8th 1955*
Algo Bueno ⎪
S.O.S. ⎭

Personnel: Victor Feldman (vibes, p, conga drum & ds) Kenny Graham (ts)
Ray Dempsey (g) Eric Peter (bs) Phil Seamen (ds, timbales, vibes) Dizzy
Reece (conga drum) Barry Morgan (maracas, timbales).

Tony Kinsey Trio with Joe Harriott   ESQUIRE EP 36

Chirracahaua ⎱ *Dec. 9th 1954*
Teddi ⎰

Personnel: Joe Harriott (as) Tony Kinsey (ds) Bill le Sage (vibes) Sammy
Stokes (bs).

Traditional Jazz Scene, 1955   DECCA LK 4100

(A) I Never Knew Just What a Girl Could Do ⎱ *Chris Barber's*
(B) St. Louis Blues   ⎬ *Jazz Band*
(A) The World Is Waiting for the Sunrise   ⎰

(C) Riverside Blues   ⎱ *The Zenith Six*
(C) Steamboat Stomp ⎰

(D) Creole Belles   ⎱ *Merseysippi Jazz Band*
(E) Young Woman's Blues ⎰

(F) Maple Leaf Rag   ⎫
(G) Black Mountain Blues ⎬ *Alex Welsh Dixielanders*
(F) Mississippi Mud   ⎭

Personnel:
(A) Chris Barber (tb) Pat Halcox (co) Monty Sunshine (cl) Lonnie Donegan
    (bj) Jim Bray (bs) Ron Bowden (ds).
(B) As (A), with Ottilie Patterson (vo).

(*C*) Tony Charlesworth (tp) Johnny Barnes (cl) Malcolm Gracie (tb) Derek Gracie (bj) Dick Lister (bs) Ron Arnold (ds).

(*D*) Pete Daniels (tp) John Lawrence (co) Don Lydiatt (cl) Frank Parr (tb) Frank Robinson (p) Ken Baldwin (bj) Dick Goodwin (bs) Trevor Carlisle (ds).

(*E*) As (*D*), with Beryl Bryden (vo).

(*F*) Alex Welsh (tp) Roy Crimmins (tb) Ian Christie (cl) Fred Hunt (p) Neville Skrimshire (g) Frank Thompson (bs) Lennie Hastings (ds).

(*G*) As (*F*), with George Melly (vo).

Scrapbook of British Jazz   DECCA LK 4139

(*A*)	Clarinet Marmalade	Oct. *1927*
(*B*)	The Mooche	May *1930*
(*C*)	Georgia On My Mind	*1934*
(*D*)	White Jazz	*1933*
(*E*)	Rosetta	Oct. *1938*
(*F*)	Royal Garden Blues	*1941*
(*G*)	Jenny's Ball	Nov. *9th 1946*
(*H*)	Black and Blue	Feb. *24th 1949*
(*J*)	Afraid of You	June *22nd 1944*
(*K*)	Skeleton Jangle	Oct. *16th 1950*
(*L*)	Early Hours	Nov. *4th 1953*
(*M*)	Bobby Shaftoe	July *13th 1954*

Personnel:

(*A*) *Fred Elizalde and his Music.* Fred Elizalde (p) Jack Jackson, Norman Payne (tps) Perley Breed (as) Jack Miranda (as & cl) Joe Crossman (ts) Joe Branelly (bj) Dick Escott (tu) Max Bacon (ds).

(*B*) *Spike Hughes' Orchestra.* Spike Hughes (bs) Max Goldberg (tp) Danny Polo (cl) Philip Buchel (as) Stan Andrews (vn) Eddie Carroll (p) Leslie Smith (g) Val Rosing (ds).

(*C*) *Nat Gonella.* Nat Gonella (tp & vo) Brian Lawrence (vn) Monia Liter, Eddie Carroll (p & pa) Harry Wilson (bs) Bob Dryden (ds).

(*D*) *Lew Stone and his Band.* Lew Stone directing: Alfie Noakes, Nat Gonella (tps) Lew Davis, Joe Ferrie (tbs) Joe Crossman (as & cl) Jim Easton (as) Harry Berly (ts) Ernest Ritte (bts) Monia Liter (p) Al Bowlly (g) Tiny Winters (bs) Bill Harty (ds).

(*E*) *George Chisholm and his Jive Five.* George Chisholm (tb) Tommy McQuater (tp) Benny Winestone (cl & ts) Eddie Macaulay (p) Tiny Winters (bs) Dudley Barker (ds).

(*F*) *Sid Phillips Quintet.* Sid Phillips (cl) Arthur Birkly (ts) Leslie "Jiver" Hutchinson (tp) Yorke de Sousa (p) Max Abrams (ds).

(*G*) *George Webb and his Dixielanders.* George Webb (p) Owen Bryce, Reg Rigden (cos) Wally Fawkes (cl) Eddie Harvey (tb) Buddy Vallis (bj) Art Streatfield (tu) Roy Wykes (ds).

(*H*) *Mark White's Jazz Club.* Freddy Randall (tp) Freddy Gardner, Cliff Townshend, Bruce Turner (cls) Geoff Love (tb) Laurie Gold (ts) Dill Jones (p) Vic Lewis (g) Hank Hobsen (bs) Max Abrams (ds).

(*J*) *George Shearing.* George Shearing (p) with unknown rhythm accompaniment.

(*K*) *Harry Gold and his Pieces of Eight.* Freddy Tomasso (tp) Ted Darrah (tb) Ernie Tomasso (cl) Laurie Gold (ts) Harry Gold (bass sax) Jimmy McKnight (p) Johnny Wiltshire (g) Gerry Hawkins (bs) Sammy Herman (ds).

(*L*) Same as DECCA LF 1152 (*page* 186).

(*M*) Same as DECCA LF 1198 (*page* 184).

INDEX

A

Abbott, Derrick, 160, 189
Abraham, Morton, 23
Abrams, Max, 191, 192
Aitkin, Gus, 181
Alker, Tom, 152
Allen, Henry, 179, 181
Allen, Russ, 147
Alvis, Hayes, 181
Ambrose, Bert, 54, 67, 85
Amis, Kingsley, 150, 173
Amos, Alex, 147
Amstell, Billy, 58
Anderson, Cat, 183
Andrews, Stan, 191
Apex Jazz Band, 158
Appleby, Keith, 148
Archey, James, 181
Armit, Ian, 150, 186
Armstrong, Lil, 178
Armstrong, Louis, 26, 53, 56, 61, 62, 63, 64, 65, 69, 74, 84, 93, 94, 114, 150, 178, 179, 181, 182, 183
Arnold, Billy, 37
Arnold, Reg, 86
Arnold, Ron, 191
Ashton, Johnny, 157
Autry, Herman, 180
Ayres, Johnnie, 156

B

Bach, J. S., 49, 117, 118
Bacharach, A. L., 126
Bacon, Louis, 181
Bacon, Max, 52, 191
Bailey, Alan, 145
Bailey, Bill, 130
Baker, Brian, 79
Baldwin, Ken, 151, 191
Ball, Ronnie, 87
Ballard, Red, 180
Baquet, Achille, 23
Barbarin, Paul, 181
Barber, Chris, 79, 80, 82, 98, 106, 109, 110, 117, 130, 131, 132, 146, 153, 184, 185, 186, 187, 190
Barber, Dudley, 70
Barclay, Bob, 151
Barker, Dudley, 191
Barnes, Johnny, 191
Bartók, Bela, 107
Basie, "Count", 94, 184
Bastable, John, 146
Bates, Colin, 153
Bates, Phil, 145
Batty, Eric, 152
B.B.C. Dance Orchestra, 69, 93
Bechet, Sidney, 24, 150
Beck, Johnny, 161